SOUTH CAROLINA
SEA CREATURES

Here's what readers from around the country are saying about Johnathan Rand's *AMERICAN CHILLERS:*

"Our whole class just finished reading 'Poisonous Pythons Paralyze Pennsylvania, and it was GREAT!"
-Trent J., age 11, Pennsylvania

"I finished reading "Dangerous Dolls of Delaware in just three days! It creeped me out!
-Brittany K., age 9, Ohio

"My teacher read GHOST IN THE GRAVEYARD to us. I loved it! I can't wait to read GHOST IN THE GRAND!"
-Nicholas H., age 8, Arizona

"My brother got in trouble for reading your book after he was supposed to go to bed. He says it's your fault, because your books are so good. But he's not mad at you or anything."
-Ariel C., age 10, South Carolina

"I just finished ALIEN ANDROIDS ASSAULT ARIZONA, and it was really great!
-Tyler F., age 9, Michigan

"American Chillers is my favorite series! Can you write them faster so I don't have to wait for the next one? Thank you."
-Alex W., age 8, Washington, D.C.

"I can't stop reading AMERICAN CHILLERS! I've read every one twice, and I'm going to read them again!"
-Emily T., age 12, Wisconsin

"Our whole class listened to CREEPY CAMPFIRE CHILLERS with the lights out. It was really spooky!"

-*Erin J., age 12, Georgia*

"When you write a book about Oklahoma, write it about my city. I've lived here all my life, and it's a freaky place."

-*Justin P., age 11, Oklahoma*

"When you came to our school, you said that all of your books are true stories. I don't believe you, but I LOVE your books, anyway!"

-*Anthony H., age 11, Ohio*

"I really liked NEW YORK NINJAS! I'm going to get all of your books!"

-*Chandler L., age 10, New York*

"Every night I read your books in bed with a flashlight. You write really creepy stories!"

-*Skylar P., age 8, Michigan*

"My teacher let me borrow INVISIBLE IGUANAS OF ILLINOIS, and I just finished it! It was really, really great!"

-*Greg R., age 11, Virginia*

"I went to your website and saw your dogs. They are really cute. Why don't you write a book about them?"

-*Laura L., age 10, Arkansas*

"DANGEROUS DOLLS OF DELAWARE was so scary that I couldn't read it at night. Then I had a bad dream. That book was super-freaky!"

-*Sean F., age 9, Delaware*

"I have every single book in the CHILLERS series, and I love them!"

-Mike W., age 11, Michigan

"Your books rock!"

-Darrell D ., age 10, Minnesota

"My friend let me borrow one of your books, and now I can't stop! So far, my favorite is WISCONSIN WEREWOLVES. That was a great book!"

-Riley S., age 12, Oregon

"I read your books every single day. They're COOL!"

-Katie M., age 12, Michigan

"I just found out that the #14 book is called CREEPY CONDORS OF CALIFORNIA. That's where I live! I can't wait for this book!"

-Emilio H., age 10, California

"I have every single book that you've written, and I can't decide which one I love the most! Keep writing!"

-Jenna S., age 9, Kentucky

"I love to read your books! My brother does, too!"

-Joey B., age 12, Missouri

"I got IRON INSECTS INVADE INDIANA for my birthday, and it's AWESOME!"

-Colin T., age 10, Indiana

Don't miss these exciting, action-packed books by Johnathan Rand:

Michigan Chillers:

#1: *Mayhem on Mackinac Island*
#2: *Terror Stalks Traverse City*
#3: *Poltergeists of Petoskey*
#4: *Aliens Attack Alpena*
#5: *Gargoyles of Gaylord*
#6: *Strange Spirits of St. Ignace*
#7: *Kreepy Klowns of Kalamazoo*
#8: *Dinosaurs Destroy Detroit*
#9: *Sinister Spiders of Saginaw*
#10: *Mackinaw City Mummies*

American Chillers:

#1: *The Michigan Mega-Monsters*
#2: *Ogres of Ohio*
#3: *Florida Fog Phantoms*
#4: *New York Ninjas*
#5: *Terrible Tractors of Texas*
#6: *Invisible Iguanas of Illinois*
#7: *Wisconsin Werewolves*
#8: *Minnesota Mall Mannequins*
#9: *Iron Insects Invade Indiana*
#10: *Missouri Madhouse*
#11: *Poisonous Pythons Paralyze Pennsylvania*
#12: *Dangerous Dolls of Delaware*
#13: *Virtual Vampires of Vermont*
#14: *Creepy Condors of California*
#15: *Nebraska Nightcrawlers*
#16: *Alien Androids Assault Arizona*
#17: *South Carolina Sea Creatures*

Adventure Club series:

#1: *Ghost in the Graveyard*
#2: *Ghost in the Grand*

www.americanchillers.com

AudioCraft Publishing, Inc.
PO Box 281
Topinabee Island, MI 49791

#17: South Carolina Sea Creatures

Johnathan Rand

An AudioCraft Publishing, Inc. book

This book is a work of fiction. Names, places, characters and incidents are used fictitiously, or are products of the author's very active imagination.

Graphics layout/design consultant: Scott Beard, Straits Area Printing
Honorary graphics consultant: Chuck Beard *(we miss you, Chuck)*
Editor: Cindee Rocheleau

Book warehouse and storage facilities provided by Clarence and Dorienne's Storage, Car Rental & Shuttle Service, Topinabee Island, MI

Warehouse security provided by Salty, Abby and Lily Munster.

American Chillers #17: South Carolina Sea Creatures
Paperback edition ISBN 1-893699-71-4
Hardcover edition ISBN 1-893699-72-2

Printed in USA

First Printing - January 2005

SOUTH
CAROLINA
SEA
CREATURES

Visit the official 'American Chillers' web
site at:

www.americanchillers.com

1

Okay. The first thing you need to know about this story is that I'm not trying to scare you away from South Carolina. I've lived here my whole life, and my family vacations all over the state. We go camping at Lake Wateree, fishing at Lake Thurmond, and hiking at Hunters Island Nature Preserve.

And when it comes down to it, there really isn't anything to be afraid of. South Carolina has some alligators, which most states don't have. We also have a few poisonous snakes. Lots of states have those, and if you use a little common sense, the snakes won't bother you. There are sharks in the ocean, but I've never seen one, and I don't worry about them when I swim.

But what happened to me this past summer was different. It had nothing to do with snakes or alligators. True, what happened to me happened at the ocean, but it had nothing to do with sharks.

It had to do with *sea creatures.*

Hideous, ugly, gigantic creatures that no one had ever seen before.

But before I tell you about what happened *this* summer, it's important that you know something about what we went through *last* summer.

My name is Chad Prescott, and I live in Charleston, South Carolina. I'm twelve, and I have a sister named Michelle. She's ten, and while she can often be a real pain, most of the time she's pretty cool. She and I have the exact same color hair—brown—except hers is a lot longer than mine. She wears it in a ponytail a lot, especially when we're on vacation.

Which was where we were last summer when all of us—Mom, Dad, Michelle and I—had a horrifying experience.

We were vacationing at a place called Hilton Head Island. It's a famous place, and lots of people go there to golf, which is why we were at Hilton Head.

Michelle and I don't golf, but Mom and Dad love the sport.

On this particular day, we had gone to the beach to swim in the ocean. The day was really warm, and the white beach sand was so hot that it stung my feet. Mom and Dad stayed on beach towels beneath a big blue and white umbrella, while Michelle and I went swimming . . . just like we always did when we spent a day at the beach.

And that's when something really scary happened.

2

I remember splashing around in the shallow water. We had met some new friends, but I don't remember their names.

What I do remember is what they were telling us about the Hilton Head Water Monster.

"He's big and green and he swallows people in one gulp," one of the kids was saying as we stood in the shallow water. The cool surf licked at my knees. Seagulls wheeled above, like white kites beneath a blue sky.

"There's no such thing," I said, shaking my head. But Michelle was falling for it.

"Really?" she asked.

"Yep," another kid said, nodding. "It's true. I've seen it before."

I shook my head. "I don't believe you," I said.

"Believe what you want," the kid replied. "I'm telling you: ask around. Lots of people have seen the monster. He waits until you're not paying attention. You might be swimming, even in shallow water. You won't see the monster until it's too late."

"And then what?" Michelle asked. Her blue eyes were bulging like marbles.

"And then it grabs you," the kid said, "and pulls you under. One gulp, and you're gone."

Michelle looked positively horrified, and I didn't think it was very nice of the kids to be scaring her that way.

But they kept at it. I think they saw how frightened Michelle was, and they knew that she believed their story.

After they left, Michelle stared out at the waves rolling in. She looked worried.

"They were only trying to scare you," I told her. "There's no such thing as the Hilton Head Water Monster."

"But what if there is?" she replied.

"There just *isn't*," I said.

"But how do you know, Chad? It could be out there right now, just waiting."

"Look out there," I said. "Lots of people are swimming and having fun. Do you think they're worried about some silly water monster?"

"Maybe they don't know about it," she said.

"For gosh sakes," I said, wading into deeper water. "Come on." I turned and reached out my hand. Reluctantly, Michelle took it, and we waded out into the water.

"Those kids were just being mean," I said. "There's nothing out here. You'll see."

Soon, the water was up over our waists. A wave washed up and almost knocked us over, and Michelle spluttered and giggled.

"See?" I said, with my best *big-brother-knows-best* voice. "Nothing to worry about at all."

As soon as I uttered those words, a dark shape appeared in the water before us. It was big and wide, but the form was too dark to make out what it was. But I knew one thing:

It was moving *fast*.

Michelle screamed, but it was already too late. The enormous beast was already upon us.

3

I think that if I had the time, I would have screamed, just like Michelle had done. But the creature was moving too fast, and in the next instant I was knocked beneath the surface. Salt water filled my mouth, burned my nostrils, and stung my eyes.

But I still had Michelle's hand, and I wasn't going to let go. I held tight with all my strength as bubbles whirled about. My foot found the soft, sandy bottom and I broke the surface. I pulled Michelle to her feet. She was coughing and choking, and then she started to cry. My head snapped around, searching the water, ready to face the awful creature that was after us.

But it was gone.

"Come on!" I said urgently, leading my sister to shallow water. "Let's get out and go tell Mom and Dad!"

All around us, there were people splashing and having fun. No one else had spotted the gigantic creature . . . yet.

But I knew it was only a matter of time.

We couldn't get out of the water fast enough. When the waves were beneath our knees, we started to run. Michelle had stopped crying, but I knew that she was still scared, so I didn't let go of her hand.

When we reached the shore, we ran across the hot sand to where Mom and Dad were sitting.

"Mom! Dad!" I exclaimed. "There's something in the water!"

"A monster!" Michelle said. She turned and pointed out to sea. "It was after us! It really was!"

Mom and Dad looked concerned. They stood up and raised their hands to their foreheads to shield their eyes from the harsh midday sun.

"Right out there," I said, pointing.

"It's the Hilton Head Water Monster," Michelle said. "We met some kids that told us that the Hilton Head Water Monster can swallow you up in one gulp!"

Dad lowered his hand and looked at Michelle. "There is no such thing as the Hilton Head Water Monster," he said. "They were only trying to fool you."

"But there's something out there," Michelle protested.

"Michelle's right," I said. "Something big knocked us over."

"It was probably just a wave," Mom said. She sat down on her beach towel.

"I'm going to go to the snack bar," Dad said. "Anybody want anything?"

I was about to tell him that I wanted some lemonade, but the words never left my lips. I was interrupted by a loud commotion in the water.

Screaming.

And shouting.

The day was hot, but a cold chill raced down my spine as I realized that there was something in the sea, after all. Michelle and I had been lucky. We had escaped.

But as we stood watching the disturbance in the water, I knew that other people weren't going to be so fortunate.

4

People began running to the waters' edge to see what was going on. Even Mom stood up again, and she and Dad stared out into the sea. I wondered what was going on, and how many people had been hurt . . . or worse.

Soon, however, we found out the truth.

"It's a sea turtle!" somebody shouted. *"Get the camera!"*

A sea turtle?!?! I thought. I had never seen one before, except on television.

Mom, Dad, Michelle, and I walked to the shore. A bunch of people had gathered in waist-deep water. We waded in, and we could see the dark form of the turtle beneath the surface. Nobody got close to it, though, and the turtle just swam around for a few more moments before heading out to deeper water.

"That was your water monster," Dad said. "A sea turtle. You probably scared it more than it scared you."

In a way, I was relieved. If I hadn't known that it was a turtle, I would probably still believe that there was some monster in the waters off Hilton Head Island.

But remember: this is what happened to us last summer. *This* summer was going to be different.

A *lot* different.

This summer, we found out that sea creatures really *do* exist. And I'm not talking about the normal creatures that you would usually find in the ocean. I'm talking about giant beasts from the darkest depths of the Atlantic . . . and it all started on a cloudy, rainy day on the Isle of Palms.

The Isle of Palms is another popular place in South Carolina. As islands go, it's not far from the mainland at all. Dad and Mom have some friends who have a guest house, and they invited us to stay for two whole weeks!

I couldn't wait. I had never been to the Isle of Palms before, but I had heard that it was really cool.

We planned to go to the beach a lot, and take a chartered nature cruise.

The first day of vacation was rainy and gray. Mom and Dad were bummed because they wanted to play golf. I was bummed because Michelle and I were going to go fishing in a small wooden rowboat. Dad and Mom had said that they would allow us to use the boat as long as we wore life vests and didn't get too far from shore.

But the rain ended around noon, and Mom and Dad said we could go. It was still too wet for them to go golfing, so they decided that they would just hang out or go for a walk.

Michelle and I loaded up our fishing poles and tackle boxes. I'm not a very good fisherman, and I usually don't catch many fish, but I have a lot of fun, anyway. So does Michelle.

"I can't believe Mom and Dad are letting us go out alone," Michelle said as she slipped into her life vest.

"Well, I *am* twelve, you know," I said. "I'm old enough to take care of myself. And you, too."

"I can take care of myself," Michelle said as we pushed the wooden rowboat into the water.

"Jump in," I said. Michelle swung her leg up and got into the boat, taking the front seat. I pushed the boat out a little farther. When the water was almost to my knees, I climbed in and took my place in the back of the boat and slipped into my life vest, buckling it around my waist. Then I grasped the oars and dipped the blades into the water.

"Maybe we'll see another sea turtle like last year," Michelle said as she leaned over the side of the boat and peered into the water.

"Maybe," I said. "But I'd rather catch a fish."

But deep down, I knew that we probably wouldn't catch fish. Salt water fishing is a lot different that fresh water fishing. We didn't even have the right equipment for salt water fishing—but I didn't mind. I was just happy to be on vacation.

I rowed the boat out until the water was about four feet deep. Then I let the oars dangle in the water from the oar locks, picked up my fishing pole, and gave it a cast. Michelle was too busy looking down into the water to care about fishing.

"I can see fish right below me," she said. "Maybe you should fish here."

"Those are just little ones," I said. "I want to catch bigger ones than that."

I wouldn't have to wait long. It would only be a few more casts before I had my first fish on the line.

At least, I *thought* it was a fish.

But that's not what it turned out to be . . . and that's how the first day of our two week vacation turned into a nightmare.

5

Michelle was leaning over the side of the boat, dragging her finger in the water. I had just made a cast. The lure arced up and plopped into the sea, and I began to reel it in.

Suddenly, the tip of my rod bent down. The rod was almost ripped out of my hands!

"Hey!" I said, grabbing the bent pole with both hands. "I've got something!"

Michelle sat up and looked to where my line vanished into the dark blue water.

"I've . . . I've got something!" I repeated, struggling to hold on to the fishing pole. "It's huge! Get the net!"

Michelle spun on the seat and picked up the net. Then she stared down into the water, looking for the fish that I was trying to reel in.

And that's when I realized something.

I *wasn't* reeling the fish in . . . he was taking more and more line out!

"What is it?" Michelle asked. "Is it a shark?"

"I . . . don't . . . know," I replied, struggling to speak as I gripped the pole. "But it's . . . it's gigantic! It's pulling the boat around!"

"It might be a whale," Michelle said.

Well, *that* was doubtful . . . but it sure *felt* like it could be a whale! One thing was certain: I'd never had a fish on the line that was this big! I couldn't wait to see what it was.

But the battle went on and on, and the only thing I could do was keep a tight grip on my fishing pole and hope that the line didn't break.

Meanwhile, the sky grew darker and darker. We hadn't been paying attention, and another storm had moved in. The wind kicked up, and the waves grew bigger. Rain began to fall.

"Can you reel that thing in already?" Michelle complained.

"I'm trying," I replied. "But this thing is big!"

"But we're a long ways from the shore," Michelle said.

I turned and looked. Michelle was right: the fish had pulled us out to sea . . . farther than we should have been.

A wave slammed into the side of the boat, knocking Michelle from her seat. "Hey!" she said as she scrambled back to the seat. "This isn't fun!"

Another wave hit the boat, causing me to lurch back. I didn't fall, but the sudden jolt was enough to jar the rod in my hand . . . and break the line.

"Oh, man!" I exclaimed angrily. "That would have been the biggest fish I've ever caught in my life!"

Another sudden gust of wind rolled the boat, and I had to grab the oars to keep myself from falling off the seat.

Only then did I realize the dangerous situation we were in. Dark clouds had closed in, and the waves were capped with white foam. We had drifted far north of the Isle of Palms, closer to Dewees Island. From where we were, I couldn't even see the beach where we'd launched the boat.

Without warning, an enormous fish exploded out of the water forty feet from where we were . . . but it only took an instant to realize that it wasn't a fish at all.

Michelle screamed. Her hands flew up to cover her mouth.

A giant, snake-like thing, bigger than our boat, rocketed up into the air and splashed back down. It was purple colored, and it looked awful. And I could see my fishing lure dangling from its mouth!

"What . . . what was that . . . that . . . *thing?*" Michelle stammered.

"It's what I was reeling in," I said, dumbfounded. "Oh, man! If I would have known that I'd hooked into that thing, I would have cut the line a long time ago!"

"We've got to get out of here!" Michelle screeched. "That thing is big enough to eat us!"

I had already grabbed the oars. Problem was, we were a *long* way from where we'd come from. It would take us an hour to row back to the Isle of Palms.

"We'll go to Dewees Island," I said. "It's closer. We can call Mom and Dad from someone's house!"

I wiped the rain from my face and began to row. Mom and Dad were probably going to be really mad—but right now, that was the least of our worries. I didn't know what that thing was that had leapt into the air . . . but it didn't look friendly.

The waves were tossing the boat around like a cork. It was hard to row and stay balanced at the same time. I kept scanning the water to see any signs of the strange, purple creature, but there was none. It was gone . . . I hoped.

Slowly, we made progress. It was raining really hard now, and the wind seemed to get stronger by the minute. Michelle and I were soaked to the skin.

Soon, I could make out houses set back on the island. My plan was to go ashore on the beach, and then we'd walk up to one of the houses.

At least, that was my plan.

But plans don't always work out the way you want them to.

A wave swelled beneath us, raising our boat up. As we began to descend, however, we were tossed sideways . . . and there was nothing Michelle or I could do to hang on. We were sent flying headlong into the water as the boat capsized.

But the last thing I saw before I plunged beneath the waves was the terrible creature's head, not thirty feet away!

6

Salt water stung my eyes and burned my nostrils. I sputtered to the surface, flailing my arms to keep from going under again. I sure was glad that I was wearing my life vest!

The boat was behind me, and Michelle had surfaced right next to it.

"We've got to get to shore!" I shouted. *"I just saw that thing again!"*

We weren't very far from the beach, but it was still too deep for us to touch bottom. Michelle and I started swimming, arm over arm, crawling toward the shore. Swimming with the life vest was kind of gawky, but at least it helped me stay afloat.

I tried not to think about the awful creature that we'd seen, but it was hard not to. I kept waiting for the terrible beast to grab my legs and pull me under.

My foot hit something and I almost screamed . . . until I realized that it was sand. I stopped swimming and stood up. The water came up to my waist, and I started wading quickly toward the shore. Large waves pushed me on.

Michelle was still swimming. "Michelle!" I shouted above the crashing waves. "Stand up!"

Michelle stood up, and I grabbed her hand. Rain drove at our faces as we clumsily waded toward shore. A wave nearly knocked me over and I almost fell.

Only a few more feet, I thought as I snapped a quick glance over my shoulder. I expected to see the terrible sea creature coming after us, but all I saw were white-capped waves and dark clouds unleashing a torrent of rain.

Almost there . . . .

Finally!

We burst from the water and onto the sand, and then ran up to a line of long, tall grass. The blades whipped and churned in the wind.

"I can't believe that just happened," I said, catching my breath.

"We are going to be in a ton of trouble!" Michelle said. "Mom and Dad are going to ground us until we have gray hair!"

Michelle was right—we were going to be in a ton of trouble, that was for sure.

But it had nothing to do with Mom and Dad. It had to do with gigantic beasts from the ocean . . . which, at the moment, were a lot closer than we could have possibly imagined.

7

We stood facing the raging sea. The wind whipped and howled, but the rain seemed to be subsiding. Which didn't really matter much at the time, since we were completely soaked, anyway.

"What do you think that thing is?" Michelle asked as she pulled a lock of wet hair from her face.

"I've never seen anything like it," I replied. "Not even in books. It looked like it could have been a giant eel . . . but eels don't have legs."

"I'm glad we got away from it," she said.

We stood for a few more moments, scanning the ocean, wondering if we would see the strange creature again.

Nope.

The only thing we saw were churning waves and whitecaps.

"Come on," I said, unbuckling my life vest and slipping it off. Michelle slipped hers off, too. "Let's go up to a house and ask someone if we can borrow their phone."

Carrying our life vests, we walked up the beach and into the tall grass that grew farther inland. A couple of homes were situated a little farther back, on the other side of a few low sloping sand dunes, and that's where we headed.

"So much for our vacation," I said. "When Mom and Dad find out where we are, they're going to be *soooo* mad."

"Hey, it wasn't my fault," Michelle said as we approached a house. It was big . . . two stories, with a huge window facing the ocean. As we drew near, I could see the clouds and the stormy sea reflected in the glass.

But Michelle was right. Being that I'm the older brother, I'm the one who is supposed to be looking after her. She was with me in the boat, and it was me who was fishing and let that . . . *thing* . . . pull us away from the Isle of Palms. I should have just cut the line and let it go when I saw the storm coming.

"Well, at least *you'll* have fun for the rest of *your* vacation," I said. "I'll probably have to stay indoors for the next two weeks."

There was a boardwalk that lead up to a door. The planks were gray and weathered, soaked with rain. Many of the houses on the Isle of Palms had walkways like this one. We followed it to a porch beneath an awning and stood at the front door.

There was a white button near the doorknob, and I reached out and pressed it. I heard the faint *ding-dong* chime from somewhere inside.

We waited. No one came.

Water dripped from our life vests.

I rang the doorbell again.

Ding-dong.

And again.

Ding-dong. Ding-dong.

Still, nobody came.

"Maybe they're not home," Michelle said. "Let's try another home."

I stepped away from the house and back onto the boardwalk.

Then I stopped.

Have you ever had the feeling that you were being watched? Like someone was watching you at that very moment?

It's an eerie feeling.

That's what I felt right then, and I turned around thinking that I would see someone in the house looking out at us.

There was no one. No one was there.

But then I looked up on the roof—and a sharp sting of terror shot right through my body.

A sea creature! The same hideous, purple creature was on the roof, glaring at us . . . preparing to strike!

8

Without even thinking, I dropped my life vest and grabbed Michelle by the hand. She dropped her life vest, too, and we ran up the boardwalk a short distance. Then we leapt into the sand and began to run to another house that wasn't very far away. Tall blades of wet grass whipped at us. Our feet sank into the soggy sand, making it even harder to run. The rain had stopped, but at this point I didn't really care. We had bigger problems to worry about.

When we were in front of the house, I managed a quick glance over my shoulder.

The creature was after us, all right. It didn't appear to be moving very fast, but it was still after us, and we had to get away.

We ran to the other side of the house. I didn't see anyone around, but we ran up to the porch. I began pressing the doorbell and pounding on the door.

"Is there anyone home?!?!" I shouted. "Please! Help us!"

After a few moments of pounding and ringing the doorbell, I realized that no one was home at this house, either.

And I also knew that the sea creature was getting closer with every passing second, and we didn't have many options. We may or may not be able to outrun the creature . . . and that's not something I really wanted to find out.

"We've got to hide," I said, frantically looking around for somewhere safe. The only place that looked appealing was several thick bushes near the corner of the house. Michelle and I might be able to hide in the dense branches and leaves.

"Over there!" I pointed, and we dashed from the porch and ran through the soft, wet sand. I pushed a few branches out of the way and nestled in, and Michelle did the same. The leaves and branches were still wet from the recent rain, but I hardly noticed

44

them. After all, our clothing was still soaked. But the clouds were breaking up, and it looked like the sun might come out soon.

And one thing was certain: we found a hiding place just in time. As soon as we had crouched down in the branches, the giant sea creature came around the side of the house. He moved like a lizard on all four claws—if that's what you could call them. The creatures' feet looked to be half flipper and half claw. I'd never seen anything like it before.

And its *mouth*.

Its mouth was open, and an enormously long, snake-like tongue lolled about. There were rows of sharp teeth on its upper and lower jaws. Two long, antennae-like feelers protruded from the top of its head.

I heard Michelle gasp and I squeezed her hand, urging her to stay calm. All the while, the creature was coming closer and closer. Its head lurched from side to side, and it sniffed the air like a dog.

What if it can smell us? I wondered. *Dogs have a really keen sense of smell. What if this monster does, too?*

The beast stopped right in front of the bushes we were hiding in. Even on all fours, it was still taller than we were! My whole body tensed, and my heart was pounding so hard that I was sure that the creature would be able to hear it. Michelle let out a little whimper, but it wasn't loud enough for the strange beast to hear. She was shaking like a leaf on a tree.

Seconds passed, and the sea creature sniffed the air. Then it slowly began moving away, finally vanishing on the other side of the garage.

We waited for a few minutes without speaking. Finally, I gave Michelle's hand another squeeze.

"Stay here for minute," I whispered. *"I'll go and make sure he's gone."*

As quietly as possible, I slipped out of the bushes, warily looking around for any sign of the dreadful creature. There were tracks in the white sand: large, deep squiggles and depressions from where the beast had walked. At least I would be able to see from the tracks which direction the creature was heading.

I peeked around the side of the garage just as a blade of sunlight knifed through the clouds. I could see where the tracks went along side the house, through the sand, and toward the ocean.

Then I spotted the sea creature.

He was at the top of a low hill, heading away from us. As I watched, the creature vanished on the other side of the hill.

I ran back to Michelle.

"He's gone," I said. "At least for now. Come on."

The bushes quaked and shook, and Michelle stepped out. She had a leaf in her hair, and I reached up and plucked it out. "Where are we going to go?" she asked. "And where is everybody?"

"I don't know," I replied. "But we've got to find a phone, even if we have to go into someone's house."

"You mean *break in?*" Michelle asked.

"Of course not," I said. "But this is an emergency. If we can't find anyone at home, maybe we can find a house that is unlocked. Then we can go in and use the phone. I'm sure the owners of the home would understand."

We walked around the house and checked the doors, but they were all locked.

"Over there," I said, pointing through a row of palm trees. "There's another house over there. Let's go check it out."

There was no one home at that house, either. However, a screen door at the back porch was unlocked, and the main door was open. After calling out for a few minutes and not getting a response from anyone, I opened the screen.

"Anybody home?" I called out again. When still no one answered, I took a step inside. I felt nervous, going in to someone's home without their permission.

But, like I had told Michelle: this *was* an emergency. We had to call for help.

"Are you going to wait outside?" I asked Michelle.

"Not with that icky thing out there somewhere," she replied as she stepped into the house.

The house was big. We walked down a long hall and into an enormous kitchen.

"Hello?" I called out again, but by this time, I was pretty sure that no one was home.

And on the wall near the refrigerator . . . .

A telephone.

Finally, I thought. *This whole thing is almost over. We can call for help . . . and go home.*

Unfortunately, it wasn't going to be quite that simple.

9

I walked across the kitchen floor and picked up the phone. My joy immediately faded when there was no dial tone.

"What's wrong?" Michelle asked.

"I . . . I can't get it to work," I said. "The phones must be out."

"We can try another house," Michelle said.

So that's what we did. After making sure that the sea creature wasn't in sight, we headed down a short, gravel-type road to yet another house. Once again, no one was home. But we found an unlocked door and went inside. And once again, we were disappointed to find that the phone didn't work.

"Man, these people are messy," Michelle said, looking around the house.

She was right. Dishes and plates sat on the dining room table. Most of them still had food on them, too. And right in the middle of the table was a stack of waffles. It looked like the people who had been here were eating breakfast, and then got up and left right in the middle of the meal. There was even an empty glass on its side. Spilled orange juice pooled on the table, and some of it had dripped over the edge and onto the wood floor.

"No, they probably aren't messy people," I said, walking through the kitchen and to the dining room table. I picked up the upended orange juice glass and raised it up, inspecting it curiously. "No, they left in a hurry for some reason. They left so fast that they accidentally knocked some things over. They didn't even have the time to clean up."

"Something scared them," Michelle said softly. "I bet they got scared away."

"And I bet I know what scared them," I said. I placed the glass on the table and looked out the window. The sky had cleared, and the sun was shining. Past the white sand dunes, waves crashed the shoreline.

And not a single person was in sight.

"Now what?" Michelle asked. "The phones don't work, and there aren't any people around. How are we going to get help? How are we going to let Mom and Dad know where we are?"

"Well, at least we're safe here," I said. "At least that creature can't get us."

Just then, I heard a noise from the other end of the hall.

A *loud* noise.

And I realized for the first time that, just because we were inside a house, it didn't mean we were safe at all . . . not by a long shot.

10

I looked at Michelle, and she looked at me. We both turned our heads and looked down the hall, in the direction of where the noise had come from.

Is it possible? I wondered. *Could the sea creature have found his way inside the house? Maybe that's why everyone left in such a hurry. Maybe there's more than one creature. Maybe—*

My thought was interrupted by still another noise from down the hall. This time I flinched, and so did Michelle. She took two quiet steps toward me and stood at my side.

"What is it?" she asked.

"I don't know," I replied.

"Do . . . do you think . . . it might be one of those . . . those things?" Michelle asked.

"How should I know?" I replied. *"I heard the same thing you did."*

We stood for a moment, listening. The only thing I could hear were a few birds chirping outside, and the distant crashing of waves as they washed over the sandy shore. There were no more sounds from the hall.

Slowly, methodically, I took a step down the hall. Michelle followed close behind.

Why are we doing this? I wondered. *Why don't we just get out of here and get away?*

But the more I thought about it, the more I realized that there really wasn't any place to go. It was probably just as dangerous here in the house as it was outside. By the looks of that sea creature, if he wanted to get into any of the houses, he probably could without too much trouble.

And so we crept on, making our way down the hall, tiptoeing silently on the wood floor.

There was a bedroom on the left, and another bedroom on the right. Both were empty.

At least, that's what I *thought.*

Once again, we heard a noise. It was just a quiet shuffling, and it sounded like it came from the closet in the bedroom on the left.

I pointed, indicating to Michelle that I thought that's where the noise came from.

And once again, I had that funny feeling of being watched. I had felt it earlier, when I was on the porch. I had turned around, only to see the giant beast on the roof, glaring down at me.

Suddenly, I didn't want to be in the house anymore. I just knew that if we didn't get out right away, something awful was going to happen.

"Let's get out of here," I whispered to Michelle, and she nodded. We both turned—but it was too late. The closet door suddenly burst open. I caught a flash of purple . . . as two sea creatures attacked!

11

I shrieked and tried to run . . . but I bumped into Michelle, knocking her to the floor. Then I tripped and landed on top of her.

"Wait!" a voice cried.

Not Michelle's voice.

Certainly not *my* voice.

I rolled and turned. A girl and boy, each probably about my age, were looking at us. The girl had long, black hair, and was wearing blue jeans and a purple sweater—almost the same color as the sea creature—and she had a look of relief on her face. The boy's hair was just as black, and he was wearing swim trunks and a blue T-shirt.

"We thought you were one of those things," the girl said.

"We thought *you* were," I said, getting to my feet. Michelle stood up.

"What are you guys doing here?" the boy asked.

"We were going to use the phone to call for help," I said.

The boy and the girl shook their heads. "The phones are out all over the island," the girl said. "It's because of those creatures."

"Is this your house?" I asked.

"It's our grandparents' home," the boy replied. "I'm Derek Baker. This is my sister, Rachel. Our parents are back home in Washington. We're just here vacationing."

"I'm Chad Prescott," I said. "This is my little sister, Michelle."

Michelle shot me a nasty look. She hated to be called *little*.

"What's going on here?" I asked. "Where did those things come from?"

Rachel shook here head and shrugged. "We don't know. They showed up this morning, and the island was evacuated. Everybody left."

"You mean there's more than one creature?" Michelle gasped.

They nodded. "We don't know how many there are," Rachel replied. "But we've seen a few already."

"How come you didn't leave?" I asked. "If everyone left the island, how come you stayed?"

Rachel and Derek looked at each other. "It was sort of an accident," Derek said. "See . . . there is only one way to get to this island."

"The ferry?" I asked. Although this was my first time on Dewees island, I'd heard that you could only get to it by taking a twenty-minute ferry ride from the Isle of Palms . . . or by a boat, like we had done.

"Yeah, that's right," Derek answered, nodding. "A guy came around and told everyone about the creatures. He was really freaked out, and said that the creatures were dangerous, and that we all had to leave right then. We were supposed to go to the ferry docks on the other side of the island, but we kind of got left behind."

"When the guy came around, we were all eating breakfast," Rachel explained. "We stopped everything, and rode golf carts to the ferry dock."

"Golf carts?" Michelle asked.

Rachel nodded. "There are no cars allowed on Dewees Island," she said. "Everyone uses electric golf carts to get around. After all, the island really isn't all that big."

"But how did you get left behind?" I asked.

"When we got there, we realized that we left Scooter, our dog, behind. Our grandparents were already on the ferry boat, but Derek and I decided to go back for our dog. When we got back here, Scooter was gone."

"Your grandparents let you leave?" I asked incredulously. "Even with the creatures all around?"

Rachel looked at Derek, then back at me. "Well, not really," she replied. "We sort of snuck away. We shouldn't have done it. But I really thought that we would find Scooter and bring him to the ferry docks. But we haven't been able to find him. I hope that something awful hasn't happened."

She didn't say it, but I knew what she meant. She was hoping that the sea creatures hadn't gone after their dog.

"And by the time we made it back to the docks," Derek continued, "the ferry boat had already left. My grandpa has a fishing boat, but the weather was too bad to try and use it to get off the island. The only thing we could do was hide from the creatures, and hope that someone comes to help us."

"So it's just the four of us," Michelle said in despair.

"Until someone discovers that we're missing and comes to rescue us," Rachel said. "Which can't be long now . . . I hope."

Suddenly, there was a tremendous crash from the other end of the house. Glass shattered, and it sounded like the house was coming down.

But when we heard the terrible, animal-like screech, we knew that what had happened was worse than the house coming down.

A sea creature was attacking!

12

"This way!" Rachel shouted, urging us into the bedroom. Behind us, on the other side of the house, we could hear more crashing and shattering of glass. It sounded like the whole house was coming down!

Rachel ran to the window and pushed it open. "We can get out this way!" she exclaimed.

Derek was the first to go. He pulled himself up and over the window sill and dropped to the soft sand. Michelle was next, followed by me, then Rachel.

"We can hide over there!" Derek pointed. "On the other side of that small dune!"

"No," Rachel said. "We'll still be spotted if one of those things comes out of the ocean. Let's go to that house over there!"

She pointed, and I could make out a cream-colored house in the distance. It sat nestled within a stand of palm trees, surrounded by white sand and long blades of grass that grew up to my waist.

Without another word, the four of us began running across the sand. Derek turned and looked behind us.

"That thing is out of the house!" he exclaimed.

I snapped my head around while my feet pounded the sand. Sure enough, the creature had emerged from the house. It was headed in our direction.

Across the sand and through the wisping blades of grass we ran, not slowing until we'd reached the house. Behind us, the gigantic purple creature was still coming, but we'd put some distance between he and us.

"Where are we going to go?" I asked as we rounded the side of the house. The home was big: two stories tall, with lots of windows that faced the ocean. "I mean . . . if we go inside, won't that thing be able to get us?"

"I don't know," Rachel said. "But we couldn't stay in my grandparents' home. Not with that thing after us!"

"Well, it's still after us," Derek said as he stopped running. We had reached the other side of the house, and we all needed to catch our breaths.

All three of us.

A sudden, gripping terror caused me to snap around frantically.

"Where's Michelle?!?!" I exclaimed. *"Where is—"*

We looked behind us, across the dune, toward Rachel and Derek's grandparents' house. Somewhere, between here and there, Michelle must have fallen. Through the tall grass and the low cresting dunes, we couldn't see her.

But we could see the terrible sea creature, still coming toward us. For the moment, the three of us were safe.

The three of us.

For Michelle, I feared that it was already too late.

13

For a moment, we just stood there, peering out around the corner of the house. I kept looking for any sign of Michelle, but I didn't see her. With every passing second, my fear grew, swelling inside of me like a hot air balloon.

"She's got to be somewhere in the dunes!" I exclaimed. "Between here and your grandparents' home!"

"But that's where the creature is!" Derek said.

"We need to get its attention," I said. "We need to draw the creature from its course. Maybe Michelle is okay. Maybe she just fell."

"I can run over to the other side of the house," Rachel said. "Maybe if I draw its attention, it will follow me. That will give you time to find Michelle."

"But what if it catches you?" Derek asked.

"I can run pretty fast. I'll be okay. Besides . . . Chad's sister is out there somewhere. We've got to find her."

I watched the strange creature. It had stopped, and was standing on its hind legs, or flippers, or whatever they were. Its mouth was open and it was looking around, sniffing the air. Its tongue rolled from side to side, lashing about like a live electrical wire.

"You guys stay here," Rachel said. "I'll run down the road and try and draw the creature away. If he comes after me, you can go back and look for Michelle. Just make sure he doesn't see you, or he might change his mind about me and come after you."

Rachel turned and ran along the side of the house. In a moment, she had vanished from view. I turned back around. The sea creature was heading toward us again, and I could hear it making strange slurping sounds. I couldn't help but think that the thing sounded like it was hungry.

Suddenly, it stopped and looked away. Something had caught its attention . . . and I knew who.

Rachel.

The creature began moving again, but had changed its direction. I knew it had spotted Rachel, and it was going after her.

"It's working!" Derek hissed.

When the creature was far enough away, Derek and I bounded from the corner of the house, crouching low to conceal ourselves from the creature. We ran back through the sand, following our footprints as we rose up a low dune, back down, then up again—

Suddenly, a form came into view. Blue jeans and a red T-shirt.

Michelle!

However, one glance told me that something was very, very wrong.

Michelle was on the sand, face-first. Her arms were sprawled out, and she wasn't moving . . . and I knew right then that we were too late.

14

I gasped in horror. For a moment, it was hard to breathe. Then I exhaled and took a deep breath.

"Michelle!" I screamed, running toward her. Something awful had happened. My poor, poor sister! Sure, she could be a pain sometimes—but I would never want to see her hurt.

Suddenly—

Her head moved!

She looked up at me, and then looked around. By the time Derek and I reached her, she was kneeling, and, because her clothing was still wet, she was covered with sand. She looked like she had been rolling in flour.

"Michelle!" I repeated. "Are you okay?"

She got to her feet and began brushing sand from her clothing. "I fell," she explained. "I thought that thing was going to get me. But I pretended to be dead, and it left me alone."

"Good thinking!" I said. At that moment, I had never been happier to see my little sister. Like I said: sometimes she can really be annoying, but I certainly wouldn't want anything to ever happen to her.

Derek was looking off into the distance. The sea creature was gone . . . but so was Rachel. What she had done was brave, and she probably helped save Michelle's life. I hoped that she was okay, too.

In the next moment, my fears eased. Rachel appeared, running over a dune toward us. She was safe.

"It worked!" I exclaimed as she reached us. "Michelle fell. She played dead, and you distracted the sea creature!"

"Where did it go?" Derek asked.

"It followed me for a ways," Rachel huffed. She was out of breath. "Then it slipped into the lagoon and disappeared."

"Where is the lagoon?" I asked.

Rachel pointed. "It's over there, on the other side of a gravel road. You can't see it from here."

"Now what?" I asked.

"Let's go back to our grandparents' house," Rachel suggested. "It'll be as safe as anywhere. Besides . . . once everyone finds out that we're missing, they'll send help. It'll be the first place they look."

"Yeah," Derek said. "And maybe Scooter will be there."

We jogged through the sand, heading for the home of Rachel and Derek's grandparents. There were only a few clouds in the sky, and the sun beat down. I was hot and uncomfortable in my damp clothing, but it was better than being gobbled up by some giant sea lizard!

We walked along the boardwalk and onto the porch, entering through the front door.

"Normally, Grandma makes us take off our shoes," Derek said, "so we don't track in a lot of sand. I don't think it's going to matter now, though."

He was right about that. The hall, the kitchen, and the living rooms were fine . . . but there was a room on the other side of the house that was in shambles. The sea creature had crashed through a big window, destroying not only the glass, but part of the wall as well.

"Scooter," Derek called out. "Scoooooter."

But there was no sign of the dog.

Rachel put her hands on her hips and surveyed the destruction in her grandparents' house. "I wonder where those creatures came from," she said. "I've never seen anything like them before. Ever."

"They look like giant eels with legs," I said. "But I've never seen them before, either."

Derek spoke up. "I think I—"

He stopped short of finishing his sentence.

"You think what?" I asked.

"Never mind," he muttered. "I just want to get off this island without getting eaten up."

Just to be sure, Rachel checked the phone again. Still no dial tone. "And Grandpa took his cellular phone, too," she said. "Otherwise, we could've used that."

So, for the time being, we just stayed put. It was too dangerous to venture outside when we didn't know when or where we might encounter another one of those things. There wasn't anything we could do but wait for help to arrive.

But I also realized that the longer we waited to be rescued, there was a chance that one of those creatures might find us first.

And when the roof suddenly exploded above us, I knew that it wasn't our rescuers. A large, gaping hole formed. Bright sunlight streamed in as debris rained down.

A shadow fell over us, and we all screamed.

A sea creature had torn a hole through the roof!

15

Talk about confusion! Pieces of the roof were falling in on us, and the creature was using his flipper-like claws to make the hole bigger! It wouldn't be long before the hole was big enough for the creature to crawl through.

The four of us scattered in different directions. I ran down the hall toward the front door. Michelle darted around the table and ran into the screened-in porch. She was easily able to escape out the screen door.

Rachel ran down the opposite hall and disappeared into the bedroom. I was sure that she was going to climb out the window like we all had done a little while ago.

But Derek—well, that was a different story. Derek spun backwards to get out of the way of a large chunk of the roof that was falling, which meant that he was backed against the kitchen counter.

Which wouldn't have been so bad, except that was the exact moment that the huge sea creature plunged through the hole, landing square in the middle of the kitchen . . . blocking Derek's escape route.

Of course, I was the only one who could see this. Rachel and Michelle were already outside of the house, while I was in the foyer near the front door.

And then, Derek did an amazing thing. I thought that he was going to scream and yell in horror. And he did—sort of. But his scream wasn't a scream of terror, it was a scream of *anger*.

"I'm getting really tired of you guys!" he shouted defiantly. *"Really, really tired!"*

Then, I did something that even surprised *me:* I ran back to help him. I figured that if Derek was brave enough to face the creature all by himself, then I could be brave enough to help him.

I dashed down the hall and stopped when I reached the kitchen. The terrible creature was so big, it seemed to fill the entire room. It was hissing and clawing the air, facing Derek, who had picked up a plate of half-eaten, cold waffles.

"Take THAT!" he exclaimed as he threw the waffles—plate and all—at the creature. Which was kind of silly, I thought, since the creature had been able to tear a hole through the roof and crash through a big glass window. A plate and a few cold waffles weren't going to do anything to stop the hideous beast.

Or were they?

The plate hit the creature in the lower jaw. Several waffles flew, and the plate crashed to the wood floor. The china shattered into dozens of white slivers, each piece tinkling and scratching as they skittered across the floor.

But most curious of all was the reaction from the sea creature. It sniffed the air, and its two antennae on the top of its head swarmed about like snakes. Then it bent down and sniffed a waffle. Its long tongue prodded the morsel, until finally the creature opened its mouth and took in the entire waffle. After it was done chewing, the beast sniffed the air again, turned around, and found another waffle on the floor.

With the creature's attention focused on the waffle, Derek began to tiptoe away. I waved to get his attention. He stopped and looked at me.

The waffles, I mouthed silently, pointing at the counter. There was a plate stacked with at least a dozen waffles next to a big silver waffle maker.

Derek knew what I was getting at. I wanted him to grab the plate before he snuck off. It was a long shot, but maybe we could somehow use the waffles to keep the creatures away from us.

Quickly and quietly, he picked up the plate and began tiptoeing away. Meanwhile, the creature had found another waffle on the floor and was chewing it up. The beast was munching away, paying no attention to Derek.

When Derek reached me, I took one of the waffles from the plate and tossed it over the head of the sea creature. It landed on the floor in the living room, made one crazy, football-like bounce, and tumbled to a stop near the coffee table.

Instantly, the creature started out for the waffle, knocking over the dining room table and breaking several chairs.

"Let's go out the front door," I whispered, and the two of us quickly tiptoed down the hall and made it to the foyer without attracting the attention of the creature. I pushed the door open, and we walked outside.

But one thing we hadn't thought about:

The sea creature was *hungry*.

Waffles are *small*.

And the beast wanted *more*.

Now.

With a bloodcurdling screech the beast stormed down the hall, into the foyer, and lunged through the front door.

16

We had been shocked when the giant beast had ripped a hole through the roof . . . but that was nothing compared to the horror we felt when the thing appeared in the doorway, mouth open, jaws gnashing, tongue flicking hungrily about.

And in Derek's hands were just the things the creature was looking for:

More waffles.

Which wasn't so bad, when you think about it. After all, I would rather have the creature eating waffles than something else . . . like me!

Thinking quickly, Derek leapt from the porch and into the white sand, and I followed. Immediately, he grabbed a waffle from the plate. In the same motion he threw the square morsel into the driveway some thirty feet away.

The creature caught wind of the airborne meal and took off after it, smashing crazily out the front door. The beast was so big that I thought it was going to get stuck, but then I remembered how easily it had ripped a hole in the roof. Something told me that it probably wouldn't have too much trouble with the front door.

We took a few steps back. By now, the hideous thing had reached the driveway. It sniffed the ground, found the waffle, looped its tongue around it, and pulled it into its mouth.

Derek plucked another waffle from the plate and gave it a toss, harder this time, launching it nearly twice as far as he had thrown the last one. The creature caught sight of it and chased after it.

But then something unexpected happened.

While we watched, *another* sea creature appeared from a small crop of bushes and trees on the other side of the gravel road! It was snarling and sneering . . . *at the other creature!*

Soon, it became apparent that they both wanted the waffle . . . and they were willing to fight for it!

"Let's get out of here while we can!" I said to Derek. "Before they come after the whole plate!"

But as it turned out, we weren't the ones who fled. The sea creatures did. They fought and fought, rolling around, screeching and screaming. Finally, one of the creatures chased the other one off. Neither returned, but I knew it was only a matter of time.

I looked at the plate of waffles in Derek's hands—and suddenly, I had an idea.

17

"You know what?" I said to Derek.

"What?"

"The creatures love waffles," I said. "At least, it seems they like them enough to want more. Why don't we *give* them some more?"

"What do you mean?" Derek asked.

"I mean . . . why don't we make up a batch of waffles and leave them for the sea creatures to eat? If the creatures are eating the waffles, they won't be very concerned with us. That might give us time to get away."

"Yeah, but where would we go?" Derek asked.

"To the ferry docks," I said. "I mean . . . it's just too dangerous to stay here. We'll have to find a boat and try to get back to the Isle of Palms."

"But we have to find my sister and your sister," he added. "And Scooter is still missing, too."

"Michelle and Rachel can't be far," I said, scanning the dunes and the area around the house. "I'm sure they left tracks in the sand. As for Scooter . . . well, maybe he found his own way off the island. Come on."

Sure enough, we found two pairs of footprints that wound around to the other side of the house. The tracks lead through the sand and tall grass, and it wasn't long before we spotted Rachel and Michelle. They were hiding inside a small storage shed near a house. They saw us first, and burst out the door and ran up to us.

"Man, are we glad to see you guys!" Rachel exclaimed. "When we didn't see you come out of the house, we thought that the creature had gotten you."

"We went out the front door," I explained. "But we found out something important. The sea creatures like to eat waffles!"

Derek raised the plate he was holding and displayed the three remaining waffles. Rachel and

Michelle both squirreled their faces. "Waffles?" Michelle said. "What's the big deal about waffles?"

"Well, in the first place," I began, "I'd rather have them eating *waffles* than eating *us*. For whatever reason, the sea creatures seem to like to eat waffles. What I told Derek was that if we made a bunch of waffles, we could leave them outside in front of the house. Hopefully, that would attract the creatures. They seem to have a pretty good sense of smell."

"What?!?!" Rachel exclaimed. "Why would you want to *attract* them?!?!"

"To give us time to get to the ferry docks," I replied. "It's too dangerous to stay here. We don't know how many creatures there are."

"Yes, we do," Derek said, hanging his head sheepishly.

"What do you mean?" I asked.

Derek raised his head. He looked at me, then at Michelle, then his sister. Then he looked back at me.

"Promise not to get mad?" he asked.

"What?" I urged. "What's going on?"

"Yeah," Rachel quizzed. "What's going on?"

Derek took a breath . . . and shared the terrible secret that he'd been keeping.

18

"Have you ever heard of sea weasels?" Derek asked.

I nodded. I've seen sea weasels advertised in the back of my comic books. They're supposed to be some type of small sea creature that you can raise in your house in a bowl of water or an aquarium. I think that they're really just shrimp or some other sort of bug. 'Sea weasels' is just a fancy name for them.

"Well, I ordered them," Derek continued. He dug his hands into his pockets and stared shamefaced down at the ground. "The directions said that it was easy to grow them and easy to take care of them."

"What does that have to do with these sea creatures?" Rachel asked. "My friend Sarah raised sea weasels. I didn't see them, but she said that they only grow to about an inch long."

Derek looked up. "I'm getting to that part," he said. "I started growing the sea weasels from the eggs that came in the kit."

"You mean that bowl of water you had in your bedroom at Grandma and Grandpa's house?" Rachel asked.

"Yeah," Derek replied. "I brought the sea weasel growing kit with us from Washington. It was in my suitcase. Grandpa gave me a bowl that I could use, and in just a few days, the sea weasel eggs hatched. Everything was going great . . . until I moved the bowl of water into the garage. That's where I had a little accident."

He paused and looked at each of us. I began to realize what he was getting at.

"Grandma has a jar of Super-Grow plant food. She says you can't use it on plants outside, because of island regulations. But you can use it on indoor plants. Well, the jar of Super-Grow was on a shelf above my bowl of sea weasels. I accidentally knocked it off the shelf . . . and a bunch of it spilled into the bowl. A couple of hours later, it looked like the sea weasels were dying . . . so I took the bowl down to the ocean and poured the dead sea weasels in."

Rachel's jaw fell. "When . . . when did you do this?" she stammered.

"Just a few days ago," Derek replied.

A heavy feeling fell over me. My arms felt like they were made of lead. Suddenly, I realized what Derek was saying. The sea weasels that he'd grown hadn't died at all . . . they'd grown to monstrous proportions. *Derek had accidentally created the sea creatures that were threatening Dewees Island!*

"The sea creatures look just like the little creatures I was raising in the bowl," Derek continued, "only now they're a lot bigger."

"How many of them are there?" Michelle asked. She had been listening intently, her eyes wide.

"Twelve," Derek replied somberly.

"Twelve?!?!" Rachel and I cried in unison. Michelle gasped and covered her mouth with her hands.

Again, Derek nodded, and he looked really ashamed. "Honest, guys . . . I didn't mean to do it. When I first saw one of the creatures, I didn't believe it. And I didn't tell anyone, because I thought I would get into trouble."

"Yeah," I said, "but if you told someone about it, maybe they could have helped. Instead, everyone left the island."

"And we're stranded here with those things," Michelle piped up.

"They could be anywhere," Rachel said.

And Rachel was right. They *could* be anywhere. In fact, we had been so wrapped up in listening to Derek's story that we weren't paying attention to what was going on around us.

And that's when one of the awful creatures attacked.

19

It happened so suddenly that all four of us screamed. From behind the shed—the very shed where Rachel and Michelle had been hiding—the giant monster lunged, making an awful screech. It must have crept up on us while we weren't paying attention.

The beast charged. It's mouth was wide and its tongue lashed out.

"To my grandparents' house!" Derek shouted, and he threw a waffle toward the sea creature. The morsel went over the creature's head, but it caught its scent and turned around to chase after it.

"To Grandpa and Grandma's!" Derek repeated. Which didn't sound very safe, since we knew that the creatures could tear down the walls and get to us if they wanted.

But we were left with no other choice. We had to run somewhere . . . and Derek's grandparents' home was the closest.

The four of us broke into a run, racing across the sand. Derek dropped the plate, but carried a waffle in each hand. We bounded up the wood boardwalk and to the porch. The front door was broken and hung from one hinge. I wondered what Derek and Rachel's grandparents would say when they saw all of the destruction in their house.

We darted inside. Derek closed the front door as best he could. "Let's get something to barricade the door!" he shouted.

We ran down the hall and into the living room. I accidentally bumped into Michelle, and she fell to the floor.

"Watch where you're going!" she fumed.

"Sorry," I replied, helping her to her feet.

A small couch sat against the far wall. "Let's use that!" Rachel said, pointing. She and Derek grabbed one end of it, while Michelle and I grabbed the other. It was heavy, and it took us nearly a full minute to drag it down the hall and wedge it against the door. Even then, I didn't think that it would stop any of the sea creatures, but it might slow them down a little, giving us a better chance to escape. Just *where* we would escape to, I had no idea. At the moment, things weren't looking too good for us.

"Now what?" Michelle asked. I was kind of wondering the same thing myself.

There was a loud crash, and the whole house shuddered.

"Does this place have a basement?!?!" I asked frantically.

"No," Rachel replied.

"But there's an attic upstairs!" Derek exclaimed. "We can hide up there!"

Without another word he spun and ran down the hall. Michelle, Rachel and I followed him as he bolted up the stairs.

"Up here!" he said, grabbing a rope that dangled from the ceiling. He pulled, and a trap door opened up. On the door itself was a folded ladder, and he grabbed one of the rungs and pulled. The ladder extended down, touching the floor.

Another loud crash from downstairs caused the entire house to tremble.

"Go!" Derek ordered, touching Michelle on the shoulder and urging her on. Michelle scampered up the ladder like a squirrel. Rachel was next, then me, then Derek. When he had climbed into the attic he turned around, grabbed the ladder, and gave it a heavy pull. The ladder retracted and folded back up, and Derek pulled the door closed. Everything went dark.

"Isn't there a light up here?" I whispered.

"There is," Rachel said, "but the bulb burned out last summer. Every day Grandma hounds Grandpa about replacing it. He always says that he'll get around to it, but probably never will."

And so, for the time being, all we could do was wait. I remembered how one of the creatures had torn a hole through the roof, and I hoped that it didn't happen again. After all, we were in the attic, and the roof was only a few feet above us. If one of those giant sea weasels decided to come after us by going through the roof . . . .

I shuddered. Maybe hiding in the attic wasn't the best thing to do, after all.

The four of us sat silently in the darkness, listening, not saying anything. Seconds turned into minutes. Finally, after not hearing any noises coming from inside the house, Rachel spoke.

"Maybe it's gone," she said quietly.

"I don't like it up here," Michelle said.

"What now?" I asked. "We can't stay up here forever."

"I'll go look," Derek said.

"But what if that thing is still down there?" Rachel asked.

"There's only one way to know for sure," Derek said. "And Chad's right. We can't stay up here forever. Sooner or later, help will come. But we can't just sit around and wait to be rescued. Hiding out in the attic worked, but we can't risk being up here if one of those things decided to come through the roof. Besides . . . I'm the one who got us into this mess. I'll go and look."

I heard shuffling, and suddenly the trap door opened downward. Light poured in, and we all squinted. Derek reached down and extended the ladder, then climbed down.

"Be careful," Rachel said.

"You sound like Mom," Derek said without looking up.

Quietly, he set a foot on the floor. Then another. He froze for a moment, listening for sounds. After a moment, he tiptoed down the hall and vanished.

We waited in the attic. Derek sure was being quiet, because we didn't hear a thing.

"The creature is probably gone," Michelle said.

But when Derek suddenly let out a bloodcurdling scream from downstairs, we knew that the creature hadn't left the house, after all.

It had been waiting . . . *and now it was attacking Derek!*

20

Derek's scream ended abruptly. Without even thinking about it, I stepped onto the ladder and descended down to the floor. Rachel was right behind me.

"Stay up there!" I ordered Michelle, and I bolted down the hall and down the stairs, afraid of what I would find on the first floor.

"Derek!" I shouted. "Are you all right?!?!"

"In here!" I heard Derek's voice echo through the house.

"Where?!?!" Rachel shouted.

"In Grandpa's den!" Derek shouted back.

I followed Rachel, and we raced down the hall and around a corner. At the end of the hall was an open door. Derek was standing in the doorway.

"Grandpa's antique desk!" he said, pointing. "The thing smashed it! Grandpa is going to go bananas!"

"That's what you screamed about?" Rachel asked, placing her hands on her hips. "We thought you were being attacked by one of those things!"

Michelle suddenly appeared around the corner, surprising us. We jumped.

"I thought I told you to wait in the attic," I said.

"You're not my boss," she replied smartly.

"No, but I'm your big brother. You have to listen to me."

She squinted and gave me a nasty look.

"Come on, you guys," Rachel said. "We have to figure something out."

The four of us walked back through the hall and into the kitchen. We looked out the windows, expecting to see one of the giant sea weasels. Thankfully, there weren't any around.

"If we can just wait long enough, help will come," Derek said. "Sooner or later, someone is going to know that we're missing. They'll come looking for us."

"I hope it's soon," Michelle said, patting her belly. "I'm getting hungry."

"How can you think of eating at a time like this?" I asked.

She shrugged. "I don't know," she said innocently. "Maybe my tummy has a mind of its own."

"Help yourself," Rachel said, nodding. "There is food in the cupboards. Eat anything you want."

"Speaking of which," I said, "we have no idea when help will arrive. We have to prepare for the worst. Let's make up a batch of waffles, and toss them out the window on the ocean side."

"But that will just attract more creatures," Rachel protested.

I nodded. "Yeah, but maybe we can distract them long enough for us to get to the ferry docks on the other side of the island."

Michelle had turned around and began opening and closing cupboard doors. She found a candy bar and was wolfing it down while she continued her search for more food.

"Chad's right," Derek said. "Waffles are easy to make. We can whip up a bunch of them in no time. Then, when we see some of the creatures coming, we can sneak out and head across the island. The house next door has an electric golf cart. We could make it to the ferry docks in just a few minutes."

Michelle was kneeling on the kitchen floor. She suddenly stood up and turned. "Too bad we couldn't use this to make the creatures smaller," she said with a smile. She was holding a large jar . . . and when I read the label, my jaw nearly hit the floor.

"Michelle!" I exclaimed. *"That's brilliant!"*

21

In Michelle's hands was a big can. The label read:

SHORTENING

"What's that stuff for?" Derek asked.

"Shortening is used for baking and frying," Rachel replied.

"But why do they call it 'shortening'?" I asked. It was a question, yes—but it was one I had the answer to.

Derek and Rachel shrugged. They didn't know.

"I bet it's because it makes things get shorter!" I exclaimed, answering my own question.

"Rachel shook her head. "I don't think that's why they call it 'shortening'."

"Well, what if it is?" I asked. My excitement was growing. "Why not try making some waffles and mixing in some shortening? Maybe the sea creatures will eat them and shrink!"

"That's silly," Michelle said.

"No it's not!" Derek said. "I read a story about a kid in Nebraska. He had to fend off giant nightcrawlers by making them shrink to normal size."

Derek's eyes lit up. "I saw that news story on television!" he exclaimed.

"But the kid in Nebraska didn't use shortening," Rachel said.

"No, but my idea is worth a shot," I said. "And the longer we wait, the more chance there is of one of those giant sea weasels attacking again. We've got to do *something.*"

"I guess it wouldn't hurt to try," Rachel said. "Let's start mixing up some waffle batter. I'll turn on the waffle iron and let it warm up."

I took the can of shortening from Michelle and opened it. Shortening is a white, greasy paste. It looked a lot like buttery ice cream. I was glad to see that the can was full.

Derek and Rachel got to work mixing up the batter in a large bowl. Then I used a spoon, scooped a large blob of shortening from the can, and plopped it into the batter, using the same spoon to mix it up.

Michelle's job was to remain on the lookout for more sea creatures . . . or a rescue team. She wandered from window to window, peering back and forth, looking all around and into the sky.

"This batch is ready," I said, handing the heavy bowl of batter to Rachel. She poured some of it into the waffle iron and closed the lid. There was a very faint hissing sound, and the air was suddenly filled with the smell of waffles. I hoped that it wouldn't attract any sea creatures. Not yet, anyway. Not until we'd made a bunch of waffles and we could use them to distract the beasts.

We were so busy working on making another batch of waffle batter that we didn't hear the strange noise until it was almost directly over us. Instantly, we knew what it was.

"A helicopter!" I exclaimed, and the three of us ran to the kitchen window. Sure enough, a helicopter was flying low over the island.

"We've got to get the pilot's attention!" Rachel exclaimed.

No sooner had she said that than Michelle appeared . . . *outside!* She, too, had heard the heavy thumping of the helicopter blades. Now she was running across the sand toward the ocean, looking up, shouting, and waving her arms like crazy, bounding through the sand and tall grass, trying to get the helicopter pilot to see her!

"Michelle! No!" I shouted. *"Come back here!"*

But she didn't hear me. She just kept running through the sand and tall grass, waving her arms, trying to get the attention of the helicopter pilot.

"I've got to get her before the sea creatures do!" I said, racing to the door that led into the screened-in porch. I bounded through the porch and outside.

"Michelle!" I shouted again. By now she was too far away. I was going to have to go and bring her back . . . and that's when I found out that we had something else to worry about.

Besides the giant sea weasels.

There was something else on the island that was just as dangerous as the sea creatures—and Michelle was just about to find out what it was.

22

South Carolina . . . Dewees Island included . . . is home to many species of snakes. Some of them are dangerous, like the Eastern Diamondback rattlesnake. It's considered the most dangerous of all rattlesnakes in North America. However, it's very rare, and, here in South Carolina, it's considered *endangered* . . . which means that there are very few of them. I've lived in South Carolina all my life, and I've never seen any.

Until today.

I was racing across the sand to find Michelle. The helicopter was fading in the distance. Obviously, the chopper hadn't been sent to rescue us, and I doubted that the pilot or anyone inside even *saw* us. If it had, I was sure that it would have turned around.

But that didn't matter right now. What mattered was finding Michelle . . . and getting her back inside the house.

When I saw her standing in the sand next to a clump of grass, I was relieved for two reasons: number one, she was okay. And number two, I didn't see any of those giant beasts anywhere.

"Michelle!" I shouted. "Come on! Get back in the house!"

She didn't respond. In fact, she didn't move at all. She was frozen, like a statue.

"Michelle?" I called out again as I walked toward her.

"Chad!" she exclaimed without moving an inch. "Help me!"

"What's wrong?" I asked, but I was close enough now to see *exactly* what was wrong.

A snake. Not just *any* old snake, either . . . a rattlesnake.

An eastern diamondback rattlesnake.

It wasn't shaking its tail and making any noise, but I knew that it didn't make any difference. It was only a foot away from Michelle, curled up in the sand and grass.

I stopped walking. "Michelle," I said, very quietly. "Don't move a muscle."

"I'm too afraid to," she replied.

"Just stay exactly as you are," I said. "Maybe he'll go away. If he doesn't think you're going to hurt him, maybe he'll just leave."

"But what if he's hungry, Chad?" Michelle asked, her voice trembling with fear. "I don't want to be eaten by a snake!" She sniffled, on the verge of crying.

"Snakes don't eat people," I said. "But he might bite you if you scare him. Just stay still. Rattlesnakes don't bite unless they think they are in danger."

I stayed right where I was, too. I didn't want the snake to see me and get frightened. One wrong move and he might bite Michelle.

"Chad!" I heard Derek shout from behind me. I turned to see him walking quickly toward us.

"Go slow," I called out to him. "We've got trouble."

Derek slowed his walk, stopping when he reached me.

"What's wrong?" he asked.

"Right there," I replied, pointing at the coiled snake near Michelle's leg. "It's an eastern diamondback rattlesnake. We'll have to wait until it goes away. If Michelle makes one move, she's a goner."

"How do you know it's an eastern diamondback?" Derek asked.

"I have a book," I said. "Those are the exact markings of an eastern diamondback. Don't scare him, and don't make him mad. We have to wait until he decides to go away."

"Or we could just catch him," Derek said.

"What?!?!?" I exclaimed in disbelief. "Derek . . . it's an eastern diamondback rattlesnake! It's the most dangerous snake around!"

"I'll bet I can catch him without getting bitten," Derek said confidently.

"You're crazy!" I said. I couldn't believe what he was saying. "You'll get bitten! Or Michelle will!"

"Oh, I don't know," Derek said. "I catch snakes like these all the time."

"You do?" I asked incredulously. "Really?"

"Sure," Derek said with a shrug. "There's nothing to it. You just have to be quick."

"You think you can catch this one?" I asked. I couldn't believe that he was actually thinking about catching a rattlesnake with his bare hands!

Derek looked at the coiled snake in the sand next to Michelle. "Yeah," he said. "I think I can. Stay here, and don't move."

I hope he knows what he's doing, I thought. *That snake is really dangerous. One wrong move . . . .*

Derek walked slowly toward Michelle, closer and closer to the coiled rattlesnake.

"Don't worry, Michelle," Derek said. "I've done this a dozen times."

When he was only a few feet away, he knelt down slowly, reaching out his hands toward the venomous serpent.

"Nice snake," he said, as if he were talking to a puppy. "Be nice. No biting."

He reached out further, his hands now inches from the snake.

"That's it," he said. "I'm not going to hurt you. I'm not going to—"

And that's when the snake struck.

23

I knew that rattlesnakes moved fast, but this one was like *lightning!* In fact, it struck so fast that I didn't even see it move!

I only saw Derek leap back, screaming and grasping his arm in pain. "He got me!" he exclaimed. "He got me! Aaaahhh!"

Michelle was scared out of her wits, and she sprang away. Thankfully, the snake didn't strike again, and Michelle escaped unharmed.

But for Derek, it was a different story. He fell to the sand, clutching his wrist. I stood there, dazed and scared, unsure of what to do. Derek had just been bitten by a venomous snake, and if he didn't go to the hospital right away . . . .

Then, Derek did something *amazing*.

Still clutching his wrist, he rolled to his knees, dangerously close to the rattlesnake. With his good arm he reached forward—

—and grabbed the diamondback by the neck!

"Bad snake!" he scolded, picking up the creature.

Wait a minute! I thought. *That . . . that snake isn't real! It's only rubber!*

"Pretty cool, huh?" Derek said with a sly grin. He held the rubber snake up and swirled it around.

"That thing is *fake?!?!*" Michelle said.

"I bought it at a gift store at the airport. I put it here the other day to see people's reactions when they walked by it. I forgot it was here."

"This isn't any time for gags!" I said angrily. "Michelle was really scared. You had me fooled, too!"

"You should have seen your face when you thought that it bit me," Derek said, looking at the snake. He seemed really proud of the prank.

"Yeah, well, at another time it might *be* funny," I replied. "But not now. Not with those . . . those *things* around here."

"Well, there aren't any right now," Derek said. "Just forget it. I thought it might be funny."

"Like I said," I answered, "it might be funny some other time. But not—"

Behind Derek, in the ocean, something moved.

Something *big*.

Michelle saw it, too. She pointed and gasped, too terrified to speak.

I caught a flash of purple.

And then a head appeared.

"Derek!" I shouted, pointing over his shoulder. *"A sea creature! It's coming out of the water!"*

Derek looked confused for a moment, but he didn't turn to see what I was pointing at.

"What?" he said. "Oh, I get it. I scared you . . . now you're trying to get me back."

"No, I'm *not!*" I exclaimed. "There really *is* a sea creature coming toward us! Come on!" I grabbed him by the arm and began to pull, but he wouldn't budge. Instead, he pulled his wrist out of my grasp and folded his arms across his chest, still holding his rubber snake. It dangled limply at his leg, and its tail touched the sand.

"Like, I'm going to believe you," he said defiantly.

"Chad's right!" Michelle screeched. "There really *is* a sea creature coming!"

"Michelle!" I ordered. "Get back to the house! Derek! Turn around and look! I'm not kidding you!

There's a sea creature coming *right now!* He's all the way out of the water!"

And it was, too. The enormous beast was walking on its hind legs. Its mouth was open, and its two peculiar antennae seemed to sniff the air.

"I told you, I'm not falling for it," Derek said. "You're just trying to get me back for scaring you with the snake."

"This is your last warning," I said, "and I'm going back to the house! Just take a look behind you, and you'll see that I'm right!"

"Oh, for crying out loud," Derek said. "All right. I'll turn—"

But by the time he actually turned to see the creature, it was too late. With a powerful lunge, the giant beast attacked.

24

I couldn't believe how fast the creature moved. In seconds, the creature was almost upon us.

Derek screamed as the enormous thing attacked. There wasn't any time to run, either. I knew already that it was too late.

Without even thinking about it, Derek threw the big rubber rattlesnake at the creature. It hit the beast in the head, then fell to the sand.

The creature stopped to sniff the snake, and it was just the break we needed. Derek and I spun at the same time, sprinting as fast as we could through the soft sand, heading for his grandparents' house. While I ran, I turned to look over my shoulder.

The sea creature had the rubber snake in its mouth and was chomping it to pieces! If Derek hadn't tossed the snake at that very moment, it would have been a different story . . . a story that wouldn't have had a happy ending.

But *our* story wasn't over quite yet. I was sure that as soon as the sea creature was finished with the snake, it would be after us again. By that time, I wanted to be as far away from the thing as possible.

Michelle had reached the house and she bounded through the screen porch, disappearing. We weren't far behind. Seconds later, Derek and I burst through the porch and into the house.

"Some of the waffles are ready!" Rachel said, pointing to a plate on the counter. "I'm making up some more right now!"

I picked up a waffle and dropped it immediately.

"Ouch!" I said, shaking my hand to cool it off. "That thing is *hot!*"

"Here's your sign," Rachel said, rolling her eyes.

"Huh?" I said. "What sign?"

"Never mind," she replied, stirring up another batch of waffle batter. "It's just an expression."

I shrugged it off and picked up the waffle with a dish towel.

"That thing is coming!" Michelle shrieked, pointing out the window. "It's coming this way!"

And it was. The creature had finished with the snake, and now it was charging toward the house.

Toward *us*.

Derek snapped up a waffle, and, forgetting that they were hot, dropped it immediately. Then he picked up a dish towel and used it to grab the waffle.

"Quick!" he exclaimed. "Let's toss these outside before he gets here!"

And we wouldn't have much time, either. The beast was rapidly approaching the house. I've seen life-like documentaries on televison about dinosaurs, and that's what the creature reminded me of: a big dinosaur.

We darted to the window, and Derek pulled back the screen. We had to be careful, because there was still a lot of junk all over the house from when one of the creatures smashed a hole through the roof.

Ignoring the heat of the waffle, I dropped the dish towel and took the morsel in my bare hand. Derek did the same, and we both tossed the waffles as far as we could. They flew for a moment, like thick, square Frisbees. Then plopped into the sand.

Meanwhile, the creature was getting closer . . . and *fast*. I crossed my fingers and hoped it would pick up the scent of the waffles.

We didn't have to wait long. The beast slowed and sniffed the air.

"He smells the waffles!" I whispered.

"Let's just hope that he finds them before he finds us," Derek whispered back.

The creature lowered its head and began to sniff the ground. After only a few seconds, it located one of the waffles. Using its tongue, it snapped up the waffle and gulped it down. Seconds later it had located the other waffle and gulped it down.

The four of us held our breath. So far, the waffles hadn't done anything to the creature.

Seconds ticked past.

Our hopes faded.

The sea creature was sniffing the ground, looking for more waffles. I knew that it was probably only a matter of moments before he picked up the scent of waffles in the house.

Then, it would be all over for us.

Unless . . . .

The sea creature stopped sniffing the ground. It had a strange look on its face, a curious expression.

Like it didn't feel well.

And then, it began changing. Problem was, it wasn't getting smaller . . . it was getting *bigger!*

Oh no! Our plan had backfired!

25

I couldn't believe my eyes.

We had hoped that by adding the shortening to the waffle that the creature would actually get smaller. Instead, the exact opposite happened. It was growing *bigger* as we watched!

"I think we're in a lot of trouble," Rachel said, as the four of us watched the creature. It was now nearly twice the size it had been.

But something even weirder happened.

Sure, the creature was getting bigger . . . but it looked awkward and bloated, like a balloon. It seemed to have trouble standing.

And if that was already hard to believe, what happened next was simply incredible.

The sea creature exploded!

There was a deep, rumbling sound, followed by a huge blast. Suddenly, the windows were caked with thick, purple goop. It began running down the windows and streaking the glass. Some of the windows were open, and the purple goop covered the screen.

"What . . . what happened?" Michelle asked quietly.

"The thing blew up!" Derek cried triumphantly. "We stopped him for good, that time!"

"Eeewww!" Michelle said, wincing.

I couldn't believe it! Although we didn't shrink the creature like we'd hoped we would, we still had succeeded in accomplishing our main goal: stopping it.

"If it worked on him," Derek said excitedly, "it'll work on the rest of them! Let's make up a bunch more waffles!"

We were energized. Now that we knew we stood a chance of stopping the sea creatures, we were hopeful that we would make it through the ordeal safely. Plus, we knew it was only a matter of time that someone would come looking for us. Perhaps the helicopter that flew over earlier had been doing just that . . . trying to find us. I was sure that Mom and Dad would've known that we were missing by now, and they would try to find us.

Unless, of course, no one was allowed on the island. Maybe it would be a long time before someone came to rescue us.

But that didn't matter now. Now, we knew how to stop the sea creatures, and that's exactly what we set out to do.

Rachel prepared the batter, while Derek and I took turns adding the shortening and stirring it up. Michelle kept a close eye on the waffle iron to make sure that none of the waffles burned.

Soon, we had over a dozen waffles made. Michelle piled them all on a plate, and the ones that didn't fit, she placed on the counter.

Rachel looked out the window toward the ocean. Her eyes widened.

"There's one!" she exclaimed. "One is coming!"

We all turned to see the creature coming toward us. Every few seconds it would stop and sniff the air, and I knew that it had picked up the scent of the waffles. We watched as the strange creature drew closer and closer with every step.

I picked up a waffle, and so did Derek.

We were ready . . . or so we *thought*.

But the sea creature did something completely unexpected . . . and I realized that our perfect plan was about to fail.

26

Derek and I had already walked to the window, ready to toss out the waffles. Creature goop covered the screen. It was really gross. Derek popped the screen out and let it fall to the ground outside.

We were just about ready to toss out the waffles when the sea creature spotted us. I didn't think it would matter, because it probably wanted the waffles more than it did us.

All of a sudden, the creature took an enormous, flying leap . . . *and landed on the roof!*

That was definitely *not* what we thought it would do. In no time at all, the creature had found the hole that one of the other creatures had created in the roof.

It was coming inside!

"Everybody out!" I screamed. *"It's coming for the waffles!"*

Derek and I climbed out the open window, still clutching our waffles. Rachel and Michelle darted out through the screened-in porch, and we met up with them in the driveway. Michelle was trembling, and so was Rachel.

"I didn't think he was going to do that!" Derek exclaimed.

"Me neither," I replied. I looked at Rachel and Michelle. "Are you guys all right?"

Michelle and Rachel nodded.

Inside the house, we could hear the creature rummaging around. It sounded like the beast was tearing down walls!

"He's looking for the plate of waffles, I bet," Derek said. "I guess that plan didn't work as well as we thought. I'm sure he's going to eat every last waffle."

"We still have these two," I said, raising the waffle I was carrying. "At least we have that much."

But then I had another thought.

The sea creature is inside the house.

The plate of waffles were in the house.

Waffles . . . with shortening.

The last sea creature that had eaten the waffles with shortening had exploded.

If a creature ate a bunch of waffles . . . .

"Take cover!" I suddenly exclaimed, grabbing Michelle by the arm.

"What?!?!" Derek exclaimed. "What?!?! Why?!?!"

But before we could run for safety, my worst fear came true.

The ground shook . . . and the entire house exploded!

27

The force of the sea creature blowing up was enough to nearly level the entire house! All around us, debris fell. Pieces of wood, part of the microwave, the refrigerator door . . . even part of the kitchen counter! Everything was covered with a film of gooey purple slime.

Luckily, nothing hit us—which was a miracle in itself. We wouldn't have had the time to get out of the way if we tried.

"Oh my gosh!" Rachel cried. "Grandpa and Grandma's house! It's completely destroyed!"

"Hey, better the house than us," Derek said, surveying the demolished house. Actually, it didn't even look like a house anymore . . . just a big pile of junk.

"Well, that's two sea creatures down, and ten to go," I said, turning the waffle over in my hand. "Problem is . . . we just lost our waffle maker. And our shortening."

"We can probably find one in a neighbor's house," Rachel suggested. "Even if we don't find a waffle iron, we could still use the batter to make pancakes. Or maybe the creatures would just eat the batter plain, without even frying it. That would be even easier."

The sun was beating down, and there wasn't a cloud in the sky. I searched for a plane or a helicopter, but there were none. There weren't even any boats at sea, which was strange. Usually, there are a lot of boats on the water . . . especially on a nice day.

"Well, whatever we do," Michelle said, "we'd better do it quick. We have only two waffles, and there are ten of those creatures left."

Without another word, we began wading through what was left of Derek and Rachel's grandparents' home. Man . . . they were in for a surprise when they were allowed back on the island!

"Keep your eyes out for those things," Derek said as we walked. "They could be anywhere."

"Where are we walking to?" Michelle asked.

"Up ahead," Rachel said, "is a house owned by friends of our grandparents. We'll go there and see if there is any waffle mix and shortening."

Problem was, to get to the house we had to walk right past the lagoon—the very lagoon where Derek had watched one of the sea creatures disappear. In the excitement of everything going on, I guess we all forgot about it.

Well, we were about to be reminded . . . in a horrible, horrible way.

28

A little bit about the lagoon:

It wasn't very big at all . . . maybe about half the size of a baseball diamond. And it didn't look to be very deep . . . maybe a few feet. Grass and reeds grew all around it. It looked really swampy, like if you were to step in it, you'd sink up to your neck.

Something in the water stirred. It was small at first, and I thought it might be a fish or maybe a frog. But then I saw two dark blue antennae emerge . . . and I knew for a fact *exactly* what it was.

Derek, Rachel and Michelle had spotted the beast, too.

"Let's try and use only one waffle and see what happens!" Derek said. "Michelle and Rachel . . . you guys go on up to the house! See if you can get inside and find some batter!"

The two girls broke into a run, racing up the white, gravelly road toward the house.

Meanwhile, it was obvious that the sea creature had spotted us. It was emerging from the water, its mouth agape, tongue lashing back and forth.

"I'll toss mine," I said, getting a solid grip on the waffle. I bent my arm inward and whipped the waffle like a Frisbee. The square piece of food spun through the air, over the lagoon—

Perfect! The creature lashed out with its tongue and snatched the waffle from the air, gulping it down without even chewing.

"Let's get out of here!" I cried. "I don't want any of that goop on me!"

We turned and followed in the footsteps of Michelle and Rachel, running as fast as we could down the gravel drive.

Suddenly, there was a loud splash behind us. Derek and I turned in time to see water and purple goop flying everywhere! It was like a car had been dropped into the lagoon! Goop covered the grass and was splattered all over the gravel road.

"Nine left!" Derek said, and we slapped high-fives. "Let's go see if Rachel and Michelle have found any waffle mix!"

Now, up until this point, we had believed that the waffles were actually destroying the sea creatures. We didn't think that they would survive after they'd eaten our special waffles mixed with shortening.

That was about to change.

Derek and I were sprinting down the road. We were almost to the driveway of the house when I heard a noise behind us.

Like claws on gravel.

I shot a glance over my shoulder . . . and was terrified to see a small purple sea creature coming after us!

29

"Derek!" I shouted. *"There's another one! He's right behind us!"*

Derek spun. By now, the small sea creature had closed the gap between us. It was only about thirty feet away.

And it wasn't very big, either. The purple creature was no taller than my knees. However, it ran much faster than the larger beasts.

It must not be all grown yet, I thought.

Derek stopped, drew his arm back, and threw the waffle. It landed on the ground in front of the creature. The small monster stopped, sniffed it a few times . . . *but it didn't eat it!*

Instead, it kept coming after us!

"Come on!" I shouted. I was just about to take off running when Derek grabbed my arm and stopped me.

"Hold on a second," he said. "There's something strange about this creature."

"They're *all* strange!" I said. "Come on! We've got to get away!"

By now, the small creature was only ten feet away, and I, too, noticed that there was something very different about this creature. Its head was different, and so were its legs.

"Wait a minute!" Derek exclaimed. "That's no sea creature! That's Scooter, our dog! He's just covered with sea creature goop! He must have been in the weeds near the water when the sea creature blew up!"

He knelt down, and the dog bounded up to him, wagging its goop-covered tail.

"Hey buddy!" Derek said. "I thought you were gone forever!"

The dog yapped happily. Derek wrapped his arm around the dog and hugged him. Creature goop smeared all over his shirt and bare arms. He even had sea creature goop on his cheek!

I darted back and picked up the waffle. "No sense in wasting this," I said, waving the square morsel in the air.

"Man, is Rachel going to be happy when she sees Scooter!" Derek exclaimed, standing up. "Even if he *is* covered with sea creature goop!"

We walked up the driveway, followed by Scooter, who looked equally happy to see Derek. The dog wagged its tail and perked its ears up. It seemed completely oblivious to the sticky goop that covered his fur.

"This is the Morrison's home," Derek explained. "They're friends of my grandma and grandpa."

"I can see movement inside the house," I said as I glanced through a window. "Rachel and Michelle are probably inside."

The front door was open, and we strode through. Sure enough, Rachel and Michelle were in the kitchen.

"We found some waffle mix!" Michelle exclaimed. "And a waffle iron, too!"

Cool! We were back in business.

"Scooter!" Rachel exclaimed as the dog bounded into the kitchen. Nails scratched the wood floor as the dog pranced around happily. Rachel dropped to the floor and gave the dog a big hug. "I thought you were gone for good!"

"Let's whip up as many waffles as we can," Derek said. "We can put them outside, at the end of the driveway. When the sea creatures come for them, they'll be in for a big surprise!"

"What if there aren't any around?" Michelle asked.

"Even better," Derek said. "I don't care if I ever see one of those things again in my life. I just hope that people are going to come looking for us soon. Then we'll be rescued."

We helped Rachel and Michelle mix the batter with shortening, then poured it into the waffle iron. As soon as they were ready, Derek and I took them outside and ran them out to the end of the driveway. In no time at all, we had a whole pile of steaming waffles in the road, and we stood by the large dining room windows to watch for the sea creatures.

We wouldn't have long to wait.

30

"There's one!" Rachel exclaimed, pointing. We all looked in the direction she was signaling.

Walking down the gravel road was a sea creature. Its head was high in the air, and it was sniffing a lot, the way a dog sniffs when it picks up a scent.

And there was no doubt that it had picked up the scent of the waffles.

"There's another one!" I exclaimed, noticing the dark purple shape emerging on the far side of the lagoon. It, too, was sniffing the air curiously, picking up the scent of the hot waffles piled in the driveway.

"I wonder if they'll get into a fight like those other two did," I said.

"We'll know in a minute," Derek replied. "Maybe some others will show up at the same time."

We watched as the two creatures ventured closer and closer. The one that was coming up the gravel road was closest to the waffles. The one on the other side of the lagoon strode into the water and was still sniffing the air, its antennae swirling about.

"They look like giant purple slugs," Michelle said with a wince. "They look icky."

The sea creature on the road reached the pile of waffles. It lowered its head to the food and took a few sniffs. Then its tongue snaked out and licked a waffle.

"What is he doing?" Rachel whispered.

"Probably just trying it out," I asked.

The creature sniffed around the pile of waffles for a few moments, then raised its head. It turned and looked in our direction, then turned around and spotted the other sea creature in the lagoon.

Suddenly, the creature on the road let out a deafening, wailing screech. It was so sudden and loud that all four of us jumped.

But the effect it had on Scooter was different. The dog had been sitting by a chair with a few pieces of purple goop still stuck to its fur. When he heard the creature's wail, he stood up on all four feet, growled, and ran to the front door. The screen was shut, but the door was open. When Scooter's nose bumped the screen door, it opened easily . . . and the dog bounded outside.

"Scooter! No!" Rachel shouted. *"Come back! Scooter!"*

But it was too late. The dog was already half way down the driveway, growling and snapping . . . heading straight for the terrible sea creature.

The beast heard the dog and turned. When it saw Scooter bearing down, it reared back and opened its mouth, exposing its long, sharp fangs.

Poor Scooter wasn't going to have a chance.

31

Scooter was running and growling, headed right for the sea creature. The terrible purple beast was waiting, its mouth open, white teeth shining in the sun.

"Scooter!" Rachel pleaded one last time.

But the dog was too focused on the sea creature.

And just when the horrible monster was about to bear down on Scooter, it suddenly turned around, letting out an awful wail at the same time.

The other sea creature had bitten its tail!

Suddenly, the two beasts were locked in battle. Scooter ran around them, barking and yipping, growling and snapping.

"Scooter!" Derek scolded. "Come here, right NOW!"

The dog suddenly stopped and looked at us, then began trotting up the driveway.

"Good boy!" Rachel exclaimed. "Come on!"

Scooter wagged his tail happily as Derek opened the screen door. The dog bounded inside.

"I know you want to protect us, buddy," Rachel said, patting Scooter on the head. "But it's too dangerous. Even for a tough dog like you." Scooter wagged his tail and sat down.

Out in the driveway, the two beasts were still fighting, rolling around, snapping at each other. I remember seeing a movie in school that had two lions fighting, and that's what the creatures reminded me of. The beasts were so vicious, so savage, it was hard to believe that they once had been harmless little sea weasels.

"Look over there!" Derek pointed.

On the other side of the lagoon, yet another sea creature was coming. It probably heard the commotion, or smelled the waffles.

"Maybe all of them will come," Michelle said. "Maybe they'll all get into fights."

"I hope not," I said. "I would rather have them eating the waffles. That way, we're sure to be rid of them."

Soon, all three beasts were fighting each other. While we watched, yet another sea creature appeared—except it didn't join in the fight. Instead, it started eating waffles!

When the other sea creatures saw this, they stopped fighting and scrambled to the pile of waffles. Then they were fighting again, trying to push each other away. They looked like hungry dogs, all trying to eat from the same bowl.

"Look at 'em go," I said. "It's like an all-you-can-eat buffet!"

Soon, one of the beasts drew away. It looked wobbly, like it was losing its balance.

"It's working!" Derek cried.

Blam!

The huge creature exploded, sending purple goop everywhere. It looked like an enormous grape had been squished at the end of the driveway.

Within seconds, the other three creatures blew up. What a mess! I wondered what people were going to say when they saw the ugly purple goop covering everything—not to mention the destruction caused to Derek and Rachel's grandparents' home.

"That makes five left," Derek said.

"The waffles are working great!" I exclaimed. "We'd better make up some more!"

Rachel and Michelle again got to work in the kitchen, making up more batter for more waffles. Derek and I kept watch around the house, making sure that no more sea creatures attacked.

One more suddenly appeared in the driveway, and it ate up the last of the remaining waffles. In minutes, it, too, had exploded.

"That leaves four," I said.

"Once that next batch of waffles is done, we'll use a golf cart and go to the ferry docks," Derek said. "If any sea creatures come after us, we can throw a waffle at them."

But as it turned out, we wouldn't be heading for the ferry docks any time soon. Right at that very moment, I heard a sound.

Derek heard it, too. Scooter, who had been laying on the floor, perked up his ears and cocked his head.

Whop-whop-whop-whop-whop . . . .

It was a fast, pulsating sound that grew louder by the second.

"The helicopter!" Derek and I shouted in unison.

We raced to a big picture window that faced the ocean, and Derek pointed.

"There it is!" he exclaimed. "Right there! He sees us!"

Rachel and Michelle joined us at the window. While we watched, the helicopter descended lower and lower.

"We're rescued!" Michelle exclaimed. "We're going home!"

The helicopter had almost landed. The blades thumped the air, and sand was sent flying. I could see the pilot inside, and he was waving, looking at us.

Rescued! We were going to be safe!

"Let's go!" I shouted over the roaring chopper blades.

"Come on, Scooter!" Rachel shouted, and the dog bounded to his feet.

We scrambled through the living room, nearly knocking each other over, heading for the door. I couldn't believe that we were finally being rescued!

Outside, the helicopter was even louder. Sand and grass was kicked up by the tremendous amount of wind that was being pushed downward by the chopper blades. We all had to squint and shield our eyes with our arms to keep the sand out. I had to squint so hard that I could hardly see.

In fact, I was squinting so hard that I didn't even see the awful creature that was lurking in the bushes near the house . . . until it was already too late.

32

The helicopter pilot was waving his hand frantically. He was shouting, too, but of course we couldn't hear him because he was inside the aircraft, and the thrumming of the blades was like thunder.

Suddenly, Michelle screamed. I turned to see the giant purple beast . . . and it was coming right for us!

The four of us all ran in different directions. I turned around and ran back to the house, quickly darting inside, through the living room, and over to the window. Michelle, thankfully, was right behind me.

"Oh my gosh!" she heaved, out of breath. "That thing almost got me!"

Outside, Derek vanished on the other side of a sand dune, and Scooter was on his heels. Rachel was running in the opposite direction, toward another house.

And the sea creature was chasing her!

"Go Rachel!" I shouted, knowing that she wouldn't be able to hear me.

"We've got to do something!" Michelle screamed. "She's not going to be able to outrun that thing!"

Michelle was right. While we watched, we could see the creature gaining on Rachel. There was no way she was going to make it—and she knew it. She glanced over her shoulder and, seeing how close the creature was behind her, changed her course, darting up a sand dune—and grabbing the trunk of a palm tree!

Meanwhile, the helicopter was rising up into the air.

"Oh no!" Michelle said. "The creature scared the helicopter away! We're not going to be rescued! Let's get some waffles and try to help Rachel!"

Michelle began to dart off, but I grabbed her by the arm. "It's too dangerous," I said. "Besides . . . look."

I pointed. Rachel was scurrying up the palm tree like a monkey. She was really fast, which was a good thing: the creature was headed right toward the same tree.

"Look!" Michelle suddenly squealed. Her arm shot out, and I looked where she was pointing.

The helicopter! It was coming back!

I had thought that the helicopter was gone, but it had only risen up into the air and circled back around. It swooped down low, heading right for the sea creature! The beast turned to get out of the way, but the helicopter pilot expertly guided the aircraft around the purple beast.

And the sea creature wasn't very happy about it, either. It was screeching and screaming like crazy.

By now, Rachel was near the top of the palm tree. She couldn't climb any higher. The only thing she could do was hang on and hope that the helicopter pilot succeeded in driving the sea creature away.

And so far, it was working. The sea creature was being driven away from the tree Rachel had climbed.

But then something terrible happened.

Worse than terrible.

What was about to happen was a catastrophe.

33

Without warning, the sea creature turned on the helicopter. The pilot didn't have time to maneuver away, and the beast suddenly grasped the chopper's landing skid! With a mighty pull, the sea creature was able to flip the helicopter sideways, causing the rotating blades to hit the sand.

It was going to crash!

In the next instant, the helicopter slammed sideways into the ground! The blades suddenly stopped whirring, and a huge cloud of sand and dust created a billowing cloud around the doomed chopper.

Thankfully, the creature didn't figure out that there was someone *inside* the helicopter. It gave the upended craft a few sniffs, and then wandered off, forgetting all about Rachel.

"We've got to help the pilot!" I exclaimed. "He might be hurt!"

"But that thing is still out there!" Michelle exclaimed.

"Yeah, but it's heading off somewhere," I said. "It might have picked up the scent of the waffles. If that's the case, we can't stay here, because—"

I was interrupted by a loud crash on the opposite end of the house. We didn't see anything, but we knew for a fact what it was.

A sea creature. It was breaking into the house!

"Let's get out of here!" Michelle shouted, and we ran to the door and bounded outside.

"To the helicopter!" I shouted. "We have to help the pilot!"

As we ran toward the crash scene, I really hoped that the pilot was all right. So far, no one had been hurt by the sea creatures. No one we knew of, anyway.

By the time we made it to the helicopter, Derek was coming back up over the sand dune, with Scooter next to him. In the distance, Rachel was scuttling down the trunk of the palm tree.

A door flung open on the sideways helicopter, and I saw a man's arm. I ran up to help.

And let me tell you, that helicopter was *big*. I guess it wasn't any bigger than any other normal-sized helicopter, but I'd never been so close to one before.

A man scrambled out the door and climbed down. He was wearing blue jeans and a military-type jacket, and a blue helmet.

"Are you all right?" I asked.

"I was going to ask you the same thing," he said. "I'm George Duncan. I came here to rescue you, but I don't think I'll be able to do that anymore."

Derek and Scooter came jogging up, followed by Rachel. Mr. Duncan introduced himself to them. Then we all started talking at once, trying to explain what had happened.

Mr. Duncan finally raised his hand. Michelle, Derek, Rachel and I were all speaking at the same time, and it was really confusing.

"Okay, okay," Mr. Duncan said. "One at a time. You say that you've found a way to stop the creatures?"

"That's right," I answered with a nod. "Waffles with shortening."

"Waffles with shortening?" Mr. Duncan asked. He looked confused. "What does *that* do?"

"It makes them blow up!" Derek said, making a gesture with his hands. "We fed a few of them a bunch

161

of waffles out in the driveway, and the creatures exploded. That's why everything on that side of the house is covered with purple goop."

"That's how I found you guys," Mr. Duncan said. "I saw a big purple stain from the sky, and I figured something had happened."

"Did you know that we were on the island?" Rachel asked.

Mr. Duncan nodded. "Yes, and your parents—and grandparents—are very worried. But we couldn't allow anyone to come and rescue you until we knew what we were dealing with."

"Giant bugs, that's what they are," Michelle piped.

"But there are only four left," Derek said.

"Four?" Mr. Duncan asked. "How do you know?"

Derek hung his head and explained how he had spilled his grandmother's plant food into the bowl of sea weasels. Mr. Duncan listened carefully.

When Derek was done explaining, Mr. Duncan peered close and looked into Derek's eyes. Then he turned to me. "How long has he been like this?" he asked.

"Like what?" I replied.

"Like this," Mr. Duncan said, pointing to Derek. "He's hysterical, and obviously in shock."

"No, he's not," Rachel said. "He's always like that."

"Well, it's just not possible for sea weasels to grow that big," Mr. Duncan said. "That's just crazy."

"That's what *I* said," Derek offered. "I thought it was crazy, too, but that's what happened."

"Well, we can figure all of that out later," Mr. Duncan said. "Right now, we've got to figure out how to get off the island."

"Doesn't your helicopter have a radio?" I asked.

"It does," Mr. Duncan replied, "but it was damaged in the crash. It won't work."

"Well, we'd better figure something out quick," Michelle suddenly said, pointing. "Because there are two of those icky things right there!"

34

We all looked where she was pointing, and saw the two purple creatures coming our way. They were on the beach, a long ways off, but they were still headed in our direction. If they hadn't spotted us yet, they would . . . and soon.

Scooter spotted the creatures, and the hair on his back went up. He growled softly. The dog still had a few blotches of goop on his fur, and he looked like a purple dalmatian.

"Quick!" Derek said. "Let's get into the house!"

"We can't!" I exclaimed. "We were just there, and we heard one of the creatures breaking in. He might still be in there!"

"Hey," Rachel said. "That gives me an idea. If there's one in the house, and those two over there, that means that there's only one other creature."

"Yeah?" I said.

"Well, if we can find a way to get rid of these three, that will make our chances of getting off the island alive a lot better. All we need to do is go and get some of those waffles that are in the house."

"But we can't go into the house," Derek said. "Not with one of those creatures in there."

"Rachel's right," I said. "If that creature is in the house, he hasn't found the waffles yet. But he will soon."

"How do you know?" Mr. Duncan asked.

"Because the whole house would have blown up," I replied. "One of us has got to go in there and get the waffles."

"I'll go," Mr. Duncan said. "It's too dangerous for you guys. Just watch out for those other two creatures. Where are the waffles?"

"On a tray on the counter," Rachel replied. "There's about a dozen of them."

We turned and looked out over the sand. The two creatures were still headed our way, but it didn't look like they'd spotted us yet.

"Hurry," Derek said, "before it's too late. And if you see the creature eating the waffles, you'd better get out of the house really fast!"

Mr. Duncan jogged up to the house and looked into the living room window.

"I don't see the creature," he said, "but the waffles are still on the counter. I'll be right back!"

He darted around the side of the house and went inside.

"I hope he hurries," Michelle said.

We didn't have to worry. In seconds, Mr. Duncan came out the door with an armload of waffles.

"He did it!" Rachel exclaimed. "He found the waffles before the creature did!"

And that's when the living room window exploded. A sea creature—the biggest one yet—attacked Mr. Duncan.

35

The shattering glass—along with the attacking creature—took all of us completely by surprise. Mostly Mr. Duncan, who was closest to the beast.

Mr. Duncan was so freaked out that he dropped most of the waffles on the ground . . . which probably saved his life. Because instead of continuing after Mr. Duncan, the creature began to gobble up the waffles.

"Run!" Rachel shouted to Mr. Duncan, who was already running as fast as he could.

Then we all took off, darting around the hulk of the crashed helicopter, heading along a sand dune toward another house. It was only a matter of time before the sea creature blew into a million globs of purple goop, and we didn't want to be anywhere nearby when it did.

But we also had to watch out for the two creatures that we'd spotted on the beach. I turned to see where they were.

"Those other two have spotted us!" I shouted as we ran. "Mr. Duncan! Drop a waffle for one of the creatures to eat!"

Mr. Duncan tossed one of the waffles over his shoulder. With any luck, one of the creatures would smell the waffle and eat it . . . and it, too, would blow up.

We heard another huge explosion as the sea creature by the house blew up. Purple goop rained down, but we were far enough away that we didn't get any on us.

"Let's get to that house over there!" Mr. Duncan ordered as we ran. "Maybe we can find someplace safe to hide until help arrives!"

We raced across the sand. Tall, thin blades of grass whipped by. Scooter remained right by Rachel's side, running along next to her.

Behind us, one of the sea creatures had gobbled up the waffle. It began running after us, but not for long. Soon, the beast stopped. Suddenly, it blew up, covering the other sea creature with purple goop.

"Drop the other waffle!" Derek said. "That other sea creature will eat it and blow himself up!"

Mr. Duncan dropped the last waffle he had, and the five of us—Scooter, too—kept running, and we never looked back . . . until we heard the sea creature explode. Then we all slowed to a stop.

"We did it!" I exclaimed, out of breath. "We got rid of the sea creatures!"

Derek shook his head. "There's still one left," he said, looking around. "He could be anywhere."

"Yeah, but if there's only one left," Mr. Duncan began, "maybe we can make it to the ferry docks without it seeing us. There's got to be a boat there, and we can use it to get off the island."

Mr. Duncan was right. With only one sea creature left, there was a good chance that we wouldn't run into it.

And besides . . . maybe the sea creature was gone. Maybe it had headed out to sea, or off to some other island. Maybe it wasn't even on Dewees island.

We jogged the rest of the way to the house. Thankfully, the garage door was open. Inside was an electric golf cart.

"Perfect," Mr. Duncan said. "Everybody climb in."

We did as he ordered. Rachel called Scooter up, and the dog jumped in and landed on her lap. Soon, we were heading out the driveway and onto the white gravel road. The further we went, the more relaxed I became.

And when the ferry docks came into view, I was happier than I'd been all day.

"There's a boat right there!" Derek said, pointing to a large rowboat moored near the ferry dock. "That's big enough for all of us! And it even has a motor on it!"

Mr. Duncan halted the golf cart, and we scrambled out. Immediately, Scooter started barking and growling at something. We all turned, and looked off toward the Isle of Palms in the distance.

And that's when we saw the big purple thing in the water, coming our way . . . *and fast.*

36

"Oh no!" Rachel cried. "There's the last sea creature! He's blocking our way!"

We watched as the beast came closer and closer.

"Wait a minute," Derek said, squinting in the sunlight. "That's . . . that's not a sea creature! That's a boat! It's a boat, and it coming toward us!"

Derek was right! The boat was a dark blue color. Because it was so far away, it only *appeared* to be a sea creature.

"You're right!" Mr. Duncan said. "It *is* a boat!"

As the vessel drew nearer, we could see people standing on it. I spotted Mom and Dad, and Michelle and I started waving.

"There's Grandpa and Grandma!" Rachel shouted. "Grandpa! Grandma!" she called out. "We're here! We're okay!"

The boat glided up to the docks. There were other people on board, too . . . including police and firemen. There were even some doctors on board, and some people who looked like they were scientists.

Suddenly, we were surrounded by people. Mom and Dad were hugging us, Rachel and Derek's grandparents were hugging them, and Scooter was running around excitedly, yipping and barking. He was just as excited as we were to be rescued.

Everyone started asking us questions at once. They all wanted to know if we were hurt, how we'd managed to survive. Derek explained exactly where the creatures came from . . . but nobody believed him!

"Really!" he insisted to a few scientists that were listening to his story. "That's exactly what happened! I spilled my grandma's jar of plant food into my bowl where I was raising sea weasels! I thought they all died, but they didn't! Instead, they grew huge!"

No matter how hard he tried, he couldn't get anyone to believe him. They refused to believe that a kid accidentally created the horrific beasts from ordinary sea weasels and plant food. Finally, Derek gave up trying to convince them.

"At least it's over," I told him.

"Not yet," Derek replied. "There is still one out there, somewhere."

"The scientists didn't believe you?" I asked.

He shook his head. "They said that there was no way that the giant sea creatures could be sea weasels. They think that it must be some sort of eel. I guess if there's anything good about this whole thing is that nobody got hurt . . . and I'm not in trouble."

We were hustled off the island on the big, dark blue boat. No one would be allowed to return to their homes on Dewees island until the scientists said that it was safe.

Derek and Rachel's grandparents had rented a motel room somewhere, but before we said goodbye, we exchanged addresses so we could keep in touch.

Michelle and I watched the news with Mom and Dad that night, and everybody was talking about the mysterious sea creatures. There wasn't any television footage of the beasts, but they showed video clips of the destruction on Dewees island, including Derek and Rachel's grandparents' demolished home. The newscaster interviewed a scientist who said that the sea creatures were probably giant eels from deep in the ocean, and that all of them appeared to be gone.

He was wrong, of course. There was one more out there. I knew it, and so did Derek.

We just didn't know where it was—until the very next morning.

37

Michelle and I were eating cereal at the table. Dad was sipping coffee, and Mom was reading the newspaper. The radio was on, and the weatherman was saying that the day was going to be sunny and very hot.

Suddenly, a woman broke in during the weather report with an urgent story. She said that a giant sea creature was attacking a hotel on Hilton Head island!

We all ran into the living room and turned on the television. We found the local news channel.

"There it is!" I exclaimed, pointing at the image on the television set. "That's one of those sea creatures! Those were the things that attacked us!"

My mom and dad couldn't believe it. While we watched, the sea creature climbed the side of the hotel. People were running everywhere, screaming, trying to stay out of the beast's way.

"If they only had some waffles with shortening, they could get rid of him," Michelle said.

"We're just glad you're home safe," Mom said, giving us each a hug. "Those things look ugly."

We watched the sea creature on television as it terrorized the poor people at the hotel. The creature didn't go inside—it just climbed up and down the side of the building. Then, without warning, it traveled back across the beach and disappeared into the sea.

So far, that's the last time the sea creature was ever spotted.

But we know that he's out there . . . somewhere.

38

Vacation ended, and we went back home. The rest of the summer flew past, and soon, school started. It was good to see all of my friends that I hadn't seen since school let out in June. I made some new friends, too.

But I missed Derek and Rachel. We'd only spent that one day with them, but so much had happened that I felt like they were my best friends.

Finally, I wrote a letter to them. I told them about the rest of my summer and the things that I did. Michelle got a puppy for her birthday, and I sent them some pictures of it.

I waited and waited to get a letter back from them, but I never did.

Finally, I just picked up the phone and called.

The phone rang for a long time. I was just about to hang up, when a man answered.

"Hello," I said. "My name is Chad Prescott. I met Derek and Rachel when they visited South Carolina this past summer."

"Oh, yes," the man said. "I'm their father."

"Is Derek there?" I asked.

"No, he's not. But Rachel is. Would you like to talk to her?"

"Yeah!" I said.

"Hang on." I heard him call for Rachel. After a moment, her voice came over the line.

"Chad?" she asked.

"Hi Rachel!" I said. "How are you?"

"Fine! Gosh! I can't believe you called! You wouldn't believe what's been going on out here!"

"Oh, I probably would," I replied. "After all, you were with us when we had to fend off those sea creatures."

"Yeah, but this is different," she said. "You're not going to believe it!"

Now I was really curious. "What's going on?" I asked.

"Well, it all started with a class field trip to a new wax museum," she replied.

"A wax museum?" I asked.

"Yeah," she answered. "It was just built. Our class had a chance to tour it before it opened."

"Cool!" I said.

"Oh, it was cool for a while," Rachel said, "until the wax figures started coming to life!"

"What?!?!" I exclaimed.

"You heard me," she said. "How much time have you got?"

"Enough for you to explain what happened," I said.

"Okay," Rachel began, "here goes."

And with that, Rachel started her story about the bizarre—and terrifying—experience that she and her friends had at the wax museum . . . .

next in the

AMERICAN CHILLERS

SERIES:

#18:

WASHINGTON WAX MUSEUM

continue on to read a few terrifying chapters!

1

"Rachel . . . can you believe they're going to let us see it first?" David asked me in a whisper. David Rydell is my next door neighbor, and he sits right behind me in class.

I shook my head. "No," I replied quietly. "It's going to be the coolest school field trip that we've ever been on!"

It was September, and school had just started. I was glad to be back. Oh, I was sorry that summer was over, but it was great to see a lot of my friends that I hadn't seen since June, when school let out for summer break.

And what a summer it had been! My brother, Derek, and I visited our grandparents in South Carolina. It's usually a lot of fun, but a really crazy thing happened: we were attacked by gigantic sea creatures! We barely escaped with our lives, and my grandparents' home was completely destroyed.

I'm sure glad *that*'s over with! I mean . . . I like a little adventure, but battling huge beasts from the sea isn't my idea of fun.

However, visiting a wax museum? Now *there* was something I could get into.

My name is Rachel Baker, and I live in Seattle, Washington. My family has lived here forever. My grandparents live here, and even my great grandparents.

And it's a great place to live. There's a lot to see and do in Seattle. Of course, Seattle is known for getting a lot of rain, but it doesn't *always* rain here. In fact, there are a lot more places in America that get more rain than we do. But there's a lot of mist and fog in Seattle, so people think that we get more rain. Not true.

And Seattle is also known for the Space Needle, which is a six hundred twenty feet tall rocket-styled building. It was built in 1962 for the World's Fair.

A lot of people are familiar with Mount St. Helens, too, which is an active volcano. It's only a couple hours' drive from Seattle.

If it sounds like I know a lot about Seattle, you're right. In fact, everyone in our class knows a lot about Seattle. You see, our school had a knowledge contest. Everyone in our class—the entire school, even—took a test to see how much they knew about our city. The class that had the best test scores won a field trip.

And not just *any* field trip.

A trip to a real wax museum!

Well, my class *won!*

But the really cool part was that we would get to visit the wax museum before it was even open to the public! Our school principal had made special arrangements with the museum director to allow us to spend a whole Saturday, seeing the wax figures and exploring the museum. Sounds fun, right?

Wrong.

Well, sure . . it *sounded* fun.

But it wasn't going to be.

And if I had thought that being attacked by sea creatures was scary, it was *nothing* compared to what was about to happen at the wax museum.

2

I was up early—before six—on that particular Saturday. David was up even earlier, and he came to the door with his backpack, ready to go.

"Come on in," I said. "Mom is making my lunch, and I have to finish my cereal."

David took a seat in the living room. "It seem like I've been waiting for this day forever!" he said.

I sat down at that kitchen table to finish my breakfast. "Me, too," I said. "I can't believe our class won the contest."

"By an inch," David said.

And he was right. Mrs. Tupper, our teacher, said that we scored ninety-seven percent . . . one percent higher than the students in Mr. Birch's class. Talk about close!

"I hope the gift store will be open," I said. "It would be cool to have a souvenir from a wax museum."

"Yeah," David agreed. "Like a little wax Frankenstein. That would be great!"

"Here's your lunch, Rachel," Mom said, placing a brown paper bag on the table. "Don't forget to put it in your backpack."

"Thanks, Mom," I said.

I finished my cereal, then I finished packing my backpack. Actually, there wasn't much that I needed to bring with me. The new wax museum was only on the other side of the city.

But we'd be there all day. Everyone was instructed to bring a lunch . . . and then we were all going out for pizza after the field trip. I also brought an umbrella, and ten dollars that I'd saved, just in case the gift store was open. And a disposable camera that Mom bought me at the department store.

"Ready?" David asked as he stood up.

"Ready," I replied, putting on my sweatshirt.

"You two have fun," Mom said, and she bent down and gave me a kiss on the cheek.

"We will, Mrs. Baker," David said with a big grin. "Today is going to be a blast! I just *know* it!"

The bus ride to the museum was boring. Although everyone was excited, it was still really early. Lots of kids slept on the bus.

Not David and me. We sat together and talked about what we might see in the wax museum. I'd never been to one before, but I saw some pictures in a book that our library has. The pictures were of wax sculptures—people—and they were really cool looking. Some of them looked so lifelike that I thought they were real.

"I hope we see a wax vampire," David said as the bus hit a bump. "You know . . . like Count Dracula or something."

"Or a werewolf!" I exclaimed. "That would be awesome!"

Finally, we arrived at the wax museum. The bus pulled into a big, open parking lot.

"Jeez, this place is empty," David said, looking out the window at the parking lot.

"It's supposed to be," I said. "The wax museum isn't open yet. We'll be the only ones here. Just us and the wax figures."

As the bus stopped, everyone got up. Half of the class was still groggy and sleepy.

"Okay everyone," Mrs. Tupper said. "Don't forget to stick together for the tour. Afterwards, you'll be allowed to buddy-up and explore the museum in groups."

"That'll be fun," I said.

"Yeah," David agreed as we shuffled along the aisle with other students, making our way toward the front of the bus. "It'll be a lot fun exploring on our own."

We got off the bus and walked across the parking lot. It was cold and windy, and the sky was iron-gray. Other students were waking up a little more, and I could feel a tingle of excitement as we got closer and closer to the door.

But I also felt something else:

Fear.

I felt a small pang of fear knotting in my belly.

Why?

It was only a wax museum, filled with wax figures.

What was there to be afraid of?

Plenty . . . as David and I were about to find out.

3

Walking into the wax museum was like walking into a big, dark room. The front doors opened up into a lobby. To the right were several ticket windows with 'closed' signs draped in front of them. To the left was the gift store. Like the ticket windows, there was a big 'closed' sign in front. Next to the sign was a wax sculpture of a man wearing old clothing. He looked like he was from the 1800s.

"Rats," David said, pointing to the closed sign. "I was really hoping the gift store would be open."

"Well, we can still take pictures," I said.

"Yeah, that'll be cool," David said.

But there was something else that was strange.

There was nobody else around.

Nobody.

The only people there were the twenty students in my class, and Mrs. Tupper, who was busy counting heads to make sure that we were all here.

"Eighteen, nineteen, twenty," she finished. "Good. We're all here. Now, I'd like everyone's attention."

We grew silent and looked at Mrs. Tupper.

"While we're here, we all need to remember a few things. First of all, the director of the wax museum has been good enough to allow our class, and our class alone, to preview the museum. Do not touch the wax figures or any other displays that you see. Does everyone understand?"

We all nodded and agreed.

"Good. I've promised the director that we'll all be on our best behavior . . ."

Mrs. Tupper continued with her instructions, but it was hard to pay attention. I guess that I was just so excited to see everything.

And then, while Mrs. Tupper was speaking, something caught my attention out of the corner of my eye.

A movement.

I looked over toward the gift store.

No, I thought. *Rachel, you're imagining things.*

" . . . and many of the things you see will surprise you," Mrs. Tupper was saying.

There!

Something moved again. I turned and looked toward the gift store.

The wax figure was gone!

4

"*David!*" I whispered as quietly as I could. Mrs. Tupper was still speaking, and I didn't want to get into trouble.

David leaned closer, but he kept his eyes forward, watching our teacher. "*What?*" he whispered.

"*That wax figure moved! It was there a minute ago, but now it's gone!*"

"*Quit kidding around,*" he said.

I shot a glance over my shoulder, just to make sure that I wasn't imagining things.

The wax figure wasn't there.

"*I'm not imagining things,*" I insisted. "*Take a look. That wax figure is gone!*"

"Miss Baker?"

Gulp.

"Yes, Mrs. Tupper?"

"Is there something you'd like to share with the class?"

"Uh, um . . . I just . . . I—"

Everyone was looking at me now, and I felt silly. My tongue felt like it was all knotted up.

"It's just that . . . well, when we came in here, there was a wax figure standing by the gift store," I said. "And now it's gone."

I turned and pointed, and received the shock of my life.

The wax figure hadn't moved at all! He was standing in the exact same spot, in the very same position that he had been!

Something really weird was going on.

"He looks like he's still there to me," Mrs. Tupper said.

Around me, my classmates were rolling their eyes and snickering. Amber Caplin frowned and gave me a nasty look. Amber has never liked me, and I don't know why. I've never done anything to her.

"Quit goofing around," she snapped quietly. *"You're going to get us all in trouble."*

I was going to say something, but I decided not to. I didn't want Mrs. Tupper mad at me.

". . . as I was saying," Mrs. Tupper continued.

I turned and glanced over my shoulder.

The wax man was still there, frozen in place.

Rachel, I thought, *you are cracking up.*

I returned my attention to Mrs. Tupper.

". . . and if the day goes well and everyone follows directions, we'll all go out for pizza before returning to the school."

Everyone began to chatter, and Mrs. Tupper raised her hands to silence us. "Remember," she said, "that's *only* if everyone follows directions."

I turned and looked behind me.

The wax figure was still there.

I shook my head, not knowing how I could have imagined such a thing.

Sheesh, I thought. *Wax figures can't move on their own.*

"The boys' restrooms are over there," Mrs. Tupper said, pointing, "and the girls' are over there. We'll take just a few minutes, and then begin the tour."

The chattering and giggling started up again as our class broke up. David wandered off, but I wanted to check something.

I wanted to see the wax man up close.

I walked over and stood near the tall figure. His skin was a little shiny, like plastic. He had black hair and a mustache, which looked very real.

I stepped closer, inspecting the figures' hand. It was the same color as human skin, except it looked glossy.

I reached my hand out, then looked around.

No one was watching. I know that Mrs. Tupper said not to touch anything, but, maybe, just this once, to satisfy my curiosity . . . .

Slowly, I reached closer. My index finger was almost touching the figures' hand.

I looked around again. Some students were peering through the windows of the gift shop, and a few more were taking turns at the drinking fountain.

I turned my attention once again to the ominous figure looming over me. The man was staring over me, beyond me. His eyes were frozen balls of wax.

Cold and lifeless.

My finger touched the back of his hand.

Suddenly the figure sprang to life! His cold hand grasped my wrist, and held on tightly.

And then I was screaming, screaming as loud as I could.

FUN FACTS ABOUT SOUTH CAROLINA:

State Capitol: Columbia

State Spider: Carolina Wolf Spider

State Nickname: The Palmetto State

State Reptile: Loggerhead Turtle

State Bird: Great Carolina Wren

State Amphibian: Spotted Salamander

State Tree: Cabbage Palmetto

State Animal: Whitetail Deer

State Flower: Yellow Jessamine

May 23rd, 1788 (8th state)

FAMOUS SOUTH CAROLINANS!

Dizzie Gillespie, jazz trumpeter

Vanna White, television personality

DuBose Heyward, poet

Strom Thurmond, politician

Joe Frazier, prize fighter

Whispering Bill Anderson, songwriter

Andrew Jackson, US president

Ertha Kitt, singer

Jesse Jackson, civil rights leader

among many, many more!

Also by Johnathan Rand:

GHOST IN THE GRAVEYARD

About the author

Johnathan Rand is the author of the best-selling **'Chillers'** series, now with over 1,500,000 copies in print. In addition to the **'Chillers'** series, Rand is also the author of the 'Adventure Club' series, including **'Ghost in the Graveyard' and 'Ghost in the Grand'**, two collections of thrilling, original short stories. When Mr. Rand and his wife are not traveling to schools and book signings, they live in a small town in northern lower Michigan with their three dogs, Abby, Salty, and Lily Munster. He still writes all of his books in the wee hours of the morning, and still submits all manuscripts by mail. He is currently working on more **'American Chillers'** and a new series of audiobooks called **'Creepy Campfire Chillers'**. His popular website features hundreds of photographs, stories, and art work. Visit:

www.americanchillers.com

For information on personal appearances,
motivational speaking engagements, or book
signings, write to:

AudioCraft Publishing, Inc.
PO Box 281
Topinabee Island, MI 49791

or call
(231) 238-0297

Join the official

AMERICAN
CHILLERS

FAN CLUB!

Visit www.americanchillers.com for details!

About the cover art: This unique cover was designed and created by Michigan artists Darrin Brege and Mark Thompson.

Darrin Brege works as an animator by day, and is now applying his talents on the internet, creating various web sites and flash animations. He attended animation school in southern California in the early nineties, and over the years has created original characters and animations for Warner Bros (Space Jam), for Hasbro (Tonka Joe Multimedia line), Universal Pictures (Bullwinkle and Fractured Fairy Tales CD Roms), and Disney. Besides art, he and his wife Karen are improv performers featured weekly at Mark Ridley's Comedy Castle over the last eight years. Improvisational comedy has provided the groundwork for a successful voice over career as well. Darrin has dozens of characters and impersonations in his portfolio. Darrin and Karen have a son named Mick.

Mark Thompson has been a professional illustrator for 25 years. He has applied his talents with toy companies Hasbro and Mattel, along with creating art for automobile companies. His work has been seen from San Diego Seaworld to Kmart stores, as well as the Detroit Tigers and the renowned 'Screams' ice-cream parlor in Hell, Michigan. Mark currently is designing holiday crafts for a local company, as well as doing website design and digital art from his home studio. He loves sci-fi and monster art, and also collects comics for a hobby. He has two boys of his own, and they're BIG Chiller Fans!

All AudioCraft books are proudly printed, bound, and manufactured in the United States of America, utilizing American resources, labor, and materials.

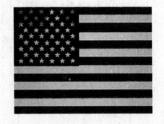

USA